Back Trails & Fishing Tales
Dave Shuffett's Outdoor Adventures

by
Dave Shuffett

Co-foreword by Joe B. Hall and
Harold Knight & David Hale

Antex Corporation
Lexington, KY 40503

An
Uncle Louie®
Publication

Copyright ©1993 by Antex Corporation. All Rights Reserved. No portion of this book may be reproduced in any form, except for brief quotations in reviews, without written permission from the publisher.

Printed in the United States of America.

ISBN 1-881079-10-4

Contributing Staff

Timothy L. Lester — Executive Editor & Managing Editor

Matthew D. Clarke — Chief Staff Assistant

John C. Stotz — Marketing Coordinator

Jennifer Bacon — Graphic Design

This book is dedicated to my wife, Diann,
and my daughter, Miranda.

A Word From the Publisher

Dave Shuffett is a man with many fine talents. As I have come to know him as publisher of his first book, *Back Trails & Fishing Tales*, I can also tell you that he is a sincere, genuine individual who was a pleasure to work with.

You will find that his excellent communication skills he demonstrates in his award-winning weekly TV show carry over into his writing.

Through Dave's leadership, *Kentucky Afield* has become one of America's most watched outdoor television shows, with ratings that have soared over the past few years.

Dave grew up in the small town of Greensburg, Kentucky, where he was exposed to hunting and fishing at an early age.

He is a 1982 graduate of Murray State University, where he got his first taste of creative writing.

Dave became host of *Kentucky Afield* in early 1989. He and his wife, Diann, have a beautiful daughter, Miranda.

I consider myself lucky for having the opportunity to work with Dave on *Back Trails & Fishing Tales*. I have gained not only an outstanding new book, but also a friend.

Timothy L. Lester, Editor

Photo Credits

Cover Photo   Alfred Fields

Additional Photos Appear Courtesy of:

Alfred Fields   Dave Shuffett

Jennifer Shuffett   Brett Billings

Diann Shuffett

Kentucky Department of Fish and Wildlife

Kentucky Educational Television

Paintings

"Sam's Rescue Attempt"   Rick Hill

"Memories of the Green"   Betty Jane Mitchell

Acknowledgments

I would like to thank my parents, Billy and Lucy Shuffett, for all their years of hard work, dedication, and patience that comes with raising a boy who did some less than intelligent things while growing up and was a little on the wild side, to put it mildly.

I'd like to acknowledge my grandparents, Ray and Easther Shuffett, whom I'll always miss. Thanks to Uncle Sam Moore, who isn't here to read the book he contributed to.

Thanks to sportsmen like Tom Stice, Ben Hall, and countless others who have taken the time to share their knowledge with me and have contributed to the show.

Thanks to Doug Hensley for encouraging me to apply for the job as host and producer of *Kentucky Afield*. Thanks, also, to former Director of Public Relations, John Wilson, and to Fish & Wildlife Commissioner Don McCormick for giving me that opportunity. And thanks to the nearly 500 employees of the Kentucky Department of Fish & Wildlife, who continually contribute to the making of the nation's oldest outdoor show.

Thanks to the best staff a fellow could ask for: Charlie Baglan, Scott Mullins and Alfred Fields of the Department of

Fish & Wildlife, and David Gibson of Kentucky Educational Television.

Special thanks to the people of Antex Corporation.

Finally, thanks to Elizabeth and Tommy Humphrey for taking in old Sam on those rare occasions when my wife and I can't be with him.

Contents

The Pact 15

Golf is a Four-Letter Word 24

The Road Back to the Outdoors 30

The Interview 33

The Initiation 38

Great Adventures 43

Technical Difficulties 76

Tall Tales 84

Old Sam and Me: A Match Made in Heaven 95

Stream Fishin' for Smallies 109

A Tradition Worth Keeping 136

Foreword

Those of us who have enjoyed the outdoor TV show, <u>Kentucky Afield</u>, on KET have witnessed Dave Shuffett's "easy" manner and captivating style in bringing us outstanding programs on hunting, fishing, and interesting aspects of the creatures and plant world around us.

Educational? Yes! But how much more! This is a beautifully told story. This is a living experience by one who has been there, touched nature with a caring and loving hand, and now tells about it in his own soft spoken, but exciting manner.

I grew up a little before Dave, but can identify with his childhood experience. My love for the outdoors and nature came about through circumstances much the same as his. Growing up in a small town, there wasn't much organized recreation for kids. We didn't have parks, swimming pools, or "little league." We had to be creative.

There were no mountains or oceans in Cynthiana, but we did have the South Licking River. Boy! What fun you can *have on a river: fishing, swimming, rope swings, boating, collecting turtles, frogs, snakes, and fishing bait (crawfish, hellgrammites, and minnows). Or you just might want to cool off on a hot summer day and have a picnic down by the dam.*

Dave has done all of these things and many, many more. He has made a business through his love of the outdoors. His every outing has been with the idea of sharing each exciting adventure with those of us who missed out, or somehow never had the opportunity to enjoy.

No one is better equipped to handle <u>Back Trails and Fishing Tales</u> than the author of this book. Interesting! Informative! Educational! Exciting! Nostalgic! Fun!

You couldn't find a better friend than Dave. He's my friend, and he'll be yours, too, after you read his book.

Joe B. Hall

Joe B. Hall
Former University of Kentucky Basketball Coach
Sr. Vice-President of Central Bank

Foreword

To host a weekly outdoor show and keep it interesting is tough enough. Dave Shuffett has been able to do just that on the <u>Kentucky Afield</u> TV series. Now he has put into words his adventures in the outdoors and the experiences of hosting this award-winning show.

We have known Dave for several years now and he is as friendly and down-to-earth in person as he is on TV. You can't help but like him.

Dave is not an overbearing person and he never claims to be an expert on his show. He's always willing to let his guests be the authority. It is this approach to television and life in general that has made him such a success.

His book will capture your attention from cover to cover with humor, folklore, true experience, hardships, and personal satisfaction.

This is one of the most enjoyable books we have read. Sit back and get ready for some heartwarming and humorous moments in Back Trails & Fishing Tales.

Your Friends,

Harold Knight   *David Hale*

Harold Knight and David Hale,
Manufacturers of Knight & Hale Game Calls, and
Hosts of the syndicated outdoor show,
Woods and Wetlands

Preface

I think you will see, as you read this book, a sincere attempt to relate to the reader a genuine sense of personal feelings on his love for the outdoors by the author. The way he shares his experiences is typical of the way he lives his life day to day. You will also feel, as you read his story, just how genuine he is in his actions. There is nothing fake or pretend about Dave. This same expression is seen by all in the *Kentucky Afield* TV show weekly. This book is a little different approach in relating to the outdoors, not your typical hunting and fishing book, and one that I think is certainly needed in this day and time.

My best to the author.

Don R. McCormick
Commissioner
Kentucky Department of Fish &
Wildlife Resources

1

The Pact

World War II Battle Scene -- Far from the Old Kentucky Home

It was a command young Billy Shuffett had not heard in the three and a half years he'd been fighting this war. "Fall back! Retreat!" screamed a nearby lieutenant. Billy couldn't believe his eyes. A wall of German Panzer tanks accompanied by thousands of foot soldiers had somehow broken through the front lines! He stumbled backward in knee-deep snow, firing his 30-caliber machine gun every few steps. But for the time being, the small arms resistance from him and his comrades was doing little good.

Hitler's final thrust was overwhelming George Patton's Third Army in this ferocious encounter that would become known as the Battle of the Bulge.

The German monstrosity would push Allied troops back fifty miles across Belgium and take thousands of American lives in the process. During the frightening retreat as he saw his comrades fall around him, Billy's mind raced with thoughts of his Kentucky home half a world away: Sunday church bells ringing on the Greensburg square, baseball games, family and friends, his mother's cooking, songbirds in chorus on a warm spring morning, and fishing on the Green River. He could just see the smallmouth bass jumping.

Billy made a pact with God that if he ever got out of that horrible place he would never again take those things for granted, and that if he ever had children he would make sure they didn't either.

Patton's forces finally halted the German offensive and 22 year-old Billy Shuffett had survived his last major battle.

Six months later he was back in his beloved Green County float fishing the Green River.

Billy Shuffett, Dave's Father

Between fishing and hunting trips, Billy worked on the family farm, sold men's clothing in his parents' dry goods store, and courted a local beauty queen who was the granddaughter of a Cherokee Indian. Billy and Audra soon married and began producing post-war baby boomers just like everybody else in the country. I came into the world on a hot August day thirteen years after the war ended. My parents later divorced and I grew up in my father's home in Greensburg, a small southern Kentucky town where everybody knew everybody: a place where "dinner" still meant the noontime meal and the pace was as slow and peaceful as the waters of Green River.

    The river flows through the heart of Greensburg, then snakes its way through the county past rolling hills dotted with farm houses and weathered barns. For many locals, the river is deep rooted in their family heritage. Since the days of the early settlers, fathers and sons have spent winter days hunting along its banks and lazy summer afternoons fishing its gentle waters. And so it was with my father and his father before him.

    This timeless tradition, coupled with the pact my father had made years before, resulted in the watery foundation of my early childhood. He would make sure I appreciated the great outdoors, never taking such awe-inspiring artistry for granted.

    I must have floated the river ten thousand times before I was six years old, as had my older siblings, Marilynn and Bill. We were encouraged not only to enjoy fishing but to notice the natural world around us: a playful grey squirrel bounding along the limb of an ancient sycamore tree, the melody of a dozen songbirds, the noble stance of a great blue heron degraded by its obnoxious call, looming boulders and their ghostly shadows cast out across the forest green water.

Artist Betty Mitchell's Rendition of Green River Memories

For those of us who spent much of our lives in the outdoors, images of natural beauty can only be outdone by images of weather extremes.

In his younger days, during the 1930's, my father would endure the worst of elemental conditions on hunting and fishing trips, and in one case, he endured extreme sickness.

It was a rainy, blustery day in December about a year before the war. Daddy had been invited to duck hunt along the river that day with his older brother-in-law, Sam Moore. The night before, his mother noticed he was a bit pale and stopped up.

"Now Billy, I don't care how long you and Sam have planned this, but you are not going duck huntin'," she said with a firm voice.

"Mother, I'm just fine," he replied. "I've just got a stopped up nose and it ain't gonna' hurt me to go huntin'."

In those days, mothers knew how important hunting and fishing excursions were to young men. She reluctantly said nothing more and kissed him goodnight on the cheek. It was one of those mistakes in judgment that mothers never forget and always blame themselves for. The next evening, young Billy came home from his hunting trip with a couple of mallards and a rapidly developing case of pneumonia. He was laid up in bed for days. He would go on to survive four years of war, but it was the icy rain on a Green River duck hunting trip that almost killed him.

DAVE SHUFFETT'S OUTDOOR ADVENTURES

In Kentucky, the harsh winds of winter turn to warm southern breezes by the middle of April, and by July, the climate makes another dramatic change. It can be excruciating. I've often pondered that hell may be just a bit hotter but probably less humid, and if there's a hell on earth, it is a Kentucky tobacco field in late August. I'll never forget those torturous days spent bent over, sweating, chopping, chopping and chopping.

It was on a sticky July day in my early years that a memorable river trip involving Sam and my father unfolded. It was one of those summer days when the slightest physical exertion caused one to break out in a soaking sweat. The leaves were as still as a photograph and the sun struggled to shine through a dingy humid sky. The birds and other wildlife along the bank had disappeared, hiding away somewhere to escape the oppressive ninety-eight degree heat. The fish were apparently doing the same thing. We had floated downstream for hours without the slightest hint of a strike when suddenly, out of nowhere, a two pound largemouth bass leaped out of the water, into our jon-boat, and into Sam's open tackle box. The confused fish thrashed around in the tackle box for a few seconds, then leaped back into the water adorned with at least six of Sam's favorite hand carved lures. In his laid-back southern drawl, Sam said, "Well, at least he's got a nice new coat of many colors."

Uncle Tommy Skaggs was another frequent companion on our outdoor excursions. He was a fidgety fellow who was always tripping over tackle boxes and sticking hooks in his finger. But Tommy could catch fish with the best of them and he was just as interested in seeing me become a good fisherman as my father was. I remember Tommy scolding me on one trip when I was seven or eight years old.

"David, I've told you three times today that you gotta' get your lure over closer to the bank where the rocks and the root wads are!" he berated as he wrapped his bleeding thumb in a handkerchief.

My brother, Bill, laughed and Daddy didn't say much of anything, which made my emotions turn from frustration to anger. But I did cast my Heddon River Runt closer to the bank and caught two smallmouth bass and a goggle eye.

When Daddy couldn't make a fishing trip because of obligations at his store, Tommy would take us himself. Off we would go down the Green in a wooden jon-boat loaded down with fishing poles, tackle boxes, and ham biscuits Aunt Marjie had made for us.

Dads can't always be there. In our case we had aunts and uncles and grandparents who made up the difference, and the three of us are forever grateful.

I was blessed to have seen the tail-end of a bygone era; a time when entire families lived their whole lives in the same county, daring not to stray from their deep-rooted ties to the land and all it bore; a time when one could still see boys strolling down dirt roads in straw hats with cane poles thrown over their shoulders; a time before the preponderance of interstate highways, urbanization and the fracturing of families; a Mayberrian image reminiscent of Andy and Opey and the whole cast of characters; images never taken for granted and forever imprinted on my soul thanks to a pact made on a battlefield in Belgium in 1944.

2

Golf is a Four-Letter Word

By the time I was eleven years old, I had become a veteran sportsman as capable as anyone, or so I thought. When they built the golf course down the road from our house I was ready to take on a new and challenging form of outdoor recreation.

My step-mother, Lucy, whom my father had married a few years earlier, had taken on the unenviable task of raising a mischievous young boy. She had actually played this game before and she was more than willing to teach me how to play. With all her good intentions, she was about to introduce me to an enemy I would battle for years to come.

Many others in our small community would become fascinated with this new sport, as well. Remember, we were a bunch of farmers, hunters and fishermen, and the only exposure most of us had to golf was occasionally through our black and white TV sets. We had seen these fellows named Palmer and Nicklaus make this strange game look easy.

"Choose Your Weapon"

But there was a myth about golf. Many of us had the preconceived notion that it was a sport for the rich. That myth was dispelled at the Green County Golf Course and Country Club. A family membership cost around two hundred and fifty dollars a year, acceptable on an installment plan. Within a year after the course was built, folks from all points in the county were rushing to join up and try this new game. Even uncles Tommy Skaggs and Sam Moore would soon spend just as much time playing golf as they did hunting and fishing.

In its early years, our golf course wasn't much to look at by today's standards. The fairways were a combination of tall fescue, rocks, and bare ground. The greens were in a little better shape, but one still had to putt across some mighty rugged terrain. And cattle were a factor. They would often escape from the adjoining farms and graze on the fescue in the fairways, which also created some excrement problems. Here and there you would see golfers cleaning it off their shoes. Sometimes a golf ball would actually land in a cow pie!

During those years, the golfers themselves looked as rugged as the course. It wasn't uncommon to see folks out on the course in overalls, flannel shirts, and work boots whaling away with every kind of unorthodox swing imaginable.

The golf course could be a dangerous place because most of the golfers, including Daddy, my brother Bill, and uncles Sam and Tommy, had mighty slices that were as dramatic and beautiful to watch as a two hundred and fifty yard drive down the middle of the fairway. These were extraordinary slices that would sometimes wind up two fairways over, putting other golfers in grave danger.

Lucy was intent on seeing me become a good player. She would say, "David, you're young enough to develop a good swing, unlike most of the adults out here." She encouraged me to practice whenever possible, even after long, grueling days of hauling hay or cutting tobacco, if daylight allowed. Lucy would also encourage me to watch the contenders in club tournaments as long as I didn't try to imitate their swings.

I remember watching the final round in our first club championship between Buster Vaughn and Cotton Bardin. I don't think either of them broke 90.

Through my early teenage years, I was spending more and more of my spare time on the golf course and less time hunting and fishing. I had developed a golf swing Lucy had become satisfied with, and sometimes my scores would reflect that.

I remember shooting an even par 72 when I was about fifteen years old. But I had trouble remaining consistent. I believe it was the very next day that I fired a blistering 92. I could never seem to conquer this frustrating enemy I had become obsessed with, but each day after work or school I would head to the golf course with a new battle strategy. When that strategy didn't work, I was quite capable of throwing a God-awful temper tantrum. I'll never forget one particular round just before my sixteenth birthday.

I had three-putted two of the first five holes for double bogeys, then on number six tee I duck-hooked my drive into the nearby practice range. My ball was lost among hundreds of range balls. At that point I stomped around, cursed a little, then threw my club for what seemed like half a mile. Daddy, who was playing along with me, became enraged with my behavior. He proceeded to give me the worst licking I've ever had in my life, right there on the number six fairway. To this day, whenever I play golf, I try to refrain from outbursts of anger.

There were other boys coming up on the golf course at the same time I was, and most of them wound up on the high school golf team. Gerald and John Gupton, Steve Graham, Mitch Theiss, the Larimore boys, and Jim Perkins were all developing into good players.

Some of them are good players today. In fact, Jim Perkins and John Gupton could give most golfers in the country a run for their money. But in those days, playing practical jokes on the older members of the country club and each other were just as important as shooting good scores against other teams.

One morning I found my clubs strung up on the golf course flag pole, a joke probably instigated by Gerald Gupton.

Another common practice was to dip up some fresh cow manure with a stick and sling it at unsuspecting teammates while their backs were turned.

I can't write this book without mentioning the great trash can caper that John Gupton and I concocted. Late one summer afternoon after a thunderstorm rolled across the golf course, John and I came up with an idea. Since no players were out on the course, we had a golden opportunity. We would place several of the large metal trash cans high up in the trees. Folks would think that storm really did some strange things. It was a lot of hard work, but it paid off. For months we would overhear club members talk about that most unusual storm, which raised up the trash cans but did no other damage. The weather sure is mysterious.

It was a prank I feel terribly guilty about today because I now realize someone had to remove all those trash cans from the trees. Oh, the foolish things we do when we're young.

I had some wonderful years on the golf course, but by the time I was nineteen years old, I was beginning to long for the peace of mind I had known years before: sunlight dancing off the water as it rushes past ancient boulders, a smallmouth bass breaking the surface, engulfing a top water lure, the sudden thrill of flushing a covey of quail. I longed for the foundation of my early youth, a foundation I would rediscover years later through an outdoor television show called *Kentucky Afield*.

3

The Road Back to the Outdoors

Who knows what happens to kids when they reach their late teens and early twenties. Besides being virtually obsessed with the opposite sex, they can also be wilder than bucking broncos. This was certainly my situation. I look back on those years with much embarrassment.

I did manage to find enough stability to make it through Murray State University with a degree in Communications.

Shortly after college I met a beautiful blonde from Louisville. The day of our first date I felt some uneasiness about the compatibility of the two of us, she being a life-long city girl and I being raised up in a town with only two stoplights. But when I knocked on Diann's door that evening, I could hear the music of Merle Haggard coming from inside. When she answered the door, I asked her how long she'd been listening to country music. She smiled and said, "Well, to tell you the truth, I was raised on it."

Later that evening, Diann told me of her own rural roots. Finding work in Louisville, her father moved the family to the city when she was a little girl. She had spent much of her life living in Louisville during the week and traveling with her family back home to their small farm house in Marion County, Kentucky, on the weekends. She often tagged along with her father and brother on hunting excursions, learning to handle rifles and shotguns exceptionally well at an early age.

I eventually married this well-rounded blonde who is perfectly at home in both the city and the backwoods. Diann would eventually become a practicing psychologist with plenty of class and sophistication, as well as the ability to take out a groundhog at 300 yards. She's my kind of woman. I just hope I never make her really mad!

One of the first things we did after the honeymoon was to buy ourselves a golden retriever puppy. We named him Yosemite Sam's Gold. Never in our wildest fancies did we realize the impact Sam would have on our lives later on.

We spent our first years together in the Appalachians, where I worked as a television news reporter first at a small station in Hazard, Kentucky, and later at an NBC affiliate in Bristol, Virginia. In the mountains I covered everything from coal mining disasters to forest fires and devastating floods, and over and over I saw the incredible courage mountain folks can find in times of trouble.

Eventually, we found our way back to Kentucky, where I landed a job as a bureau chief at WLEX-TV in Lexington. It was there that I found myself longing more and more to be in the woods or on a river, far away from city streets and human tragedy. By now, at the age of thirty, I had seen more than my share of murders, grisly wreck scenes, fatal fires, and lives turned upside down for one reason or another. These images were beginning to appear in my dreams at night. It was time to get out, but where could I go?

Little did I know I was about to embark on a new career that would change my life forever. Soon a lost soul would find himself.

DAVE SHUFFETT'S OUTDOOR ADVENTURES

4

The Interview

As a young boy, I had watched *Kentucky Afield* with my father, and I knew the show had an unusual owner, not a Jimmy Houston or a Bill Dance or a Marlin Perkins, but the Kentucky Department of Fish and Wildlife Resources. What I didn't know that morning in 1989 when I applied for the job as host and producer was that *Kentucky Afield* was one of the longest continuously running television series in America, and quite likely the oldest outdoor show, premiering on the air as a radio talk show back in the late `40's. It then found its way to a new phenomenon called television in 1953, when WAVE-TV in Louisville began airing it as a year round weekly series. The Department of Fish and Wildlife hierarchy was very proud of the show's longevity, and especially proud of all the men I had a chance at following. Ron Rhody was the first host and producer. He was a brilliant, forward-thinking department employee who conceived the idea for the television version of the show in the days when many

Americans thought television was a passing fad that had little chance of ever gaining the prominence of radio.

Ron Rhody in the Early Radio Days of <u>Kentucky Afield</u>

Rhody's foresight and prowess would effectuate his name as the father of outdoor television in America, and eventually lead him into the banking business, where he is now the worldwide Executive Vice-President of Bank of America.

Rhody's boss, Harry Towles, was also a man of great forethought. Towles believed in Rhody's crazy notion of outdoor television and pushed the idea until WAVE-TV in Louisville took a chance on it.

Ron Rhody Pioneering <u>Kentucky Afield</u> into Television

Next came Hope Carleton, who began his career as a Game Warden and somehow found his way to the *Kentucky Afield* spotlight. Hope stayed at the helm for twenty-three years, becoming a legendary host and admired sportsman.

When Hope retired, along came Jeremy Dreyer, the Wildlife Biologist and host who master-minded the show's move to Kentucky Educational Television, one of the more respected public television networks in America, a network that would give *Kentucky Afield* a prime time audience in several states.

Tim Michaels, one of Jeremy's staff members, took over as host and producer when Jeremy moved on to a new career in corporate communications. Tim's vast knowledge of television production and state of the art equipment kept the show at a high technical standard, a necessity to remain on the air at Kentucky Educational Television. Tim left to pursue a new avenue in television producing in late 1988, leaving the door open for a newcomer.

*Former Hosts of Kentucky Afield (left to right):
Hope Carleton, Jeremy Dreyer, and Tim Michaels, with Sam*

By the time Fish and Wildlife Commissioner Don McCormick finished giving me this history lesson during the interview, I was feeling awfully insignificant and nervous. Then the questions followed.

"Do you hunt and fish? Do you understand the financial contribution sportsmen have made toward wildlife restoration in America? Where would you like to take *Kentucky Afield?*"

After I answered his questions he sat there for a second with a contemplative look on his face, then said, "Well, Dave, I'm gonna' offer you this job. Good luck and welcome aboard. But don't even think you'll ever become as good a bass fisherman as I am."

5

The Initiation

In the spring of 1989 a whole new world had opened up to me. Daily planning sessions and conversations would no longer revolve around politics, murder investigations, and budget deficits. Instead, crappie fishing, turkey hunting, black bear management, and the logistics of video-taping wood duck surveys would dominate brainstorming sessions.

In June of 1989 one of those sessions led to my decision to cover an osprey restoration project, which would take me to the Delaware coast, a trip that would also include my initiation into the Department of Fish & Wildlife.

Ospreys, commonly called fish hawks, once adorned the skies over many parts of the United States until the pesticide DDT began to interfere with their ability to reproduce, drastically reducing their numbers. DDT found its way into fish, which comprise the osprey's entire diet. As a result the osprey, along with other birds of prey such as the bald eagle, would lay thin-shelled and often infertile eggs. But the banning of DDT has made it possible once again for these great hunters of the sky to thrive in America.

Osprey Nest in Delaware

Excited though I was that June morning, I was awfully uneasy about flying all the way to the marshes of the Delaware coast. That is where we had to go to pick up ten six-week-old ospreys. With a worrisome mind and a camera in hand I climbed aboard a Cessna aircraft with Wildlife Biologist David Yancy and Conservation Officer and pilot, Sgt. Chip McInnis.

Just before we took off, Chip asked David, "Have you seen my heart pills laying around here anywhere?"
"No, I sure haven't," David replied.

"Awh, I'll be fine. I don't need 'em anyway," Chip yelled as he fired up his engines.

I sat there silently in the co-pilot's seat, scared out of my mind as we barreled down the runway. Little did I know I was being set up. These guys had heard the green kid was afraid of flying.

About an hour into the flight I was becoming a little more relaxed. Chip and David had become new found friends. We talked about everything from Chip's instrument panel to how the birds were going to handle the trip back. And the view was spectacular. During a lull in the conversation I became engrossed in it. You could almost reach out and touch those billowing cumulus clouds hanging there against a sapphire blue sky. And down below, the blue-green mountain tops of the Appalachians reached up in every direction until they faded away into the vast horizon in front of us. We seemed so insignificant, tiny men crossing the boundless heavens in our tiny machine.

When I finally turned toward Chip to ask him a question about our exact whereabouts I saw the most shocking sight I'd ever seen in my life. Until now I had only heard of people being temporarily speechless, but now it was happening to me. No words would come out of my mouth. There he was, slumped over in his seat as lifeless as a dead man can be! I reached back to David, almost pulling him out of his seat trying to awaken him. Then, as I turned back toward Chip, I suddenly remembered the missing heart pills! This man really was dead! He evidently had died of a heart attack while I was looking out the window! I was just about to have a heart attack of my own when Chip took in a deep breath of air, chuckled and said, "Welcome aboard the Department of Fish and Wildlife, Dave!" David Yancy doubled over, he was laughing so hard. I laughed right along with them once I regained my composure, understanding, I suppose, that being initiated into the department by whatever means is an old tradition.

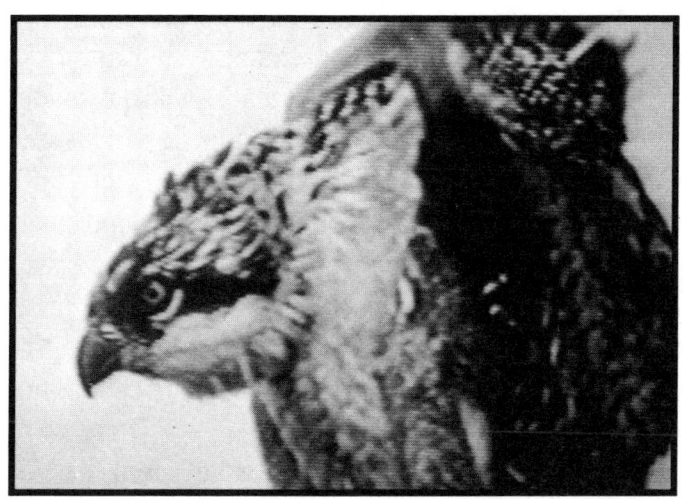

Six-week-old Osprey (taken from video)

After safely landing in Suffox County, Delaware, we hopped aboard an air boat piloted by a Delaware wildlife official and headed to the saltwater marshes near Rehoboth Beach. The osprey nests were everywhere, built on old piers, duck blinds, and in one case, the roof of a small, dilapidated house once used for a hunting camp. Through the viewfinder of my camera I noticed the young birds were lying down, motionless in their nests as David and his counterpart from Delaware approached them. They were trying to be unnoticed. Meanwhile, the adults were circling above, sometimes swooping down at us just a few feet above our heads, a situation not to be taken lightly. An adult osprey is a large bird with a wing span of four and a half to six feet.

One by one, ten young birds were carefully removed from various nests, placed in crates, and transported back to the aircraft. Dodging thunderstorms the whole way back, we flew them to Laurel River Lake in southern Kentucky where they were placed in what scientists call hacking towers, large wooden structures that serve as pseudo nesting sights. The birds eventually flew from their artificial nests, possibly as far south as Guatemala. When the ospreys journeyed back to the north two years later in preparation to raise their own young, their destination was not Delaware. They had no memory of the marshes where they were hatched. Instead, they returned to southern Kentucky, the region of their earliest memories.

The osprey project aired as a segment on *Kentucky Afield* in the early fall of 1989. Even though there were a few hair-raising seconds aboard an aircraft thanks to a couple of practical jokers, it was a great learning experience and a great adventure, the first of many more to come.

6

Great Adventures

The law of averages will certainly catch up with you if you happen to be the producer and host of a weekly outdoor show. The mishaps, the adventures, and the bizarre can quickly add up to quite a collection of tales. The following stories are a few of my favorites. And, yes, they are all true.

The Great Deer Attack

In September of 1989, I decided to do a feature on the autumn behavior of whitetail deer. It was to be a segment the deer hunters would hopefully enjoy, as well as anyone else interested in wildlife. But things didn't go quite as planned.

Wildlife Biologist Lauren Schaaf volunteered to help videographer Clint Goins and me get the feature done in an enclosed deer display area at the Kentucky Department of Fish and Wildlife headquarters complex in Frankfort, Kentucky.

Even though we were talking about wild deer populations, we needed the captive deer to get close-up shots of antler development. Bambi, as he was called, was the perfect choice. He was a healthy nine point buck, just entering the rut.

The first few minutes went fine. Lauren is a man of seemingly unending knowledge when it comes to whitetail deer. He told me about the changes a buck deer undergoes in the fall of the year, such as the swelling of the neck, the increasing in physical strength, the mood swings, and the willingness to fight other bucks, signs of the breeding season.

Lauren had just changed the subject to buck deer velvet, the hair-like substance that aids in the annual growth of antlers, when it dawned on me that Bambi had been circling us for quite some time. With each completed circle he seemed to get a little closer.

"What's that deer up to? He isn't going to charge us is he?" I asked.
"Who knows what he's up to," Lauren replied. "He's probably got other things on his mind besides eating."

That lack of confidence in Lauren's response sent me an ominous signal. But it was too late. Bambi proceeded to lower his head and charge me with all the ferocity an enraged animal can muster!

Meanwhile, Clint Goins was getting all of this on tape, doing what a good videographer is supposed to do, I guess, while the rest of us fought for our lives.

Famous Deer Attack (taken from video)

Bambi had now taken on three of us: Lauren, myself, and Johnny Widener, a nearby Fish and Wildlife employee who had seen the incident unfold and was attempting to rescue us. While Lauren ineffectively tried to flip the deer over by grabbing his back legs and pushing on his rump, Johnny and I were in a more precarious situation up front, basically dangling on his antlers. Both of us were running out of strength.

Finally, we had to let go. As soon as we did, Bambi charged me again! I took a pretty good blow to the midsection, but not bad enough to put me down. I managed, once again, to grab hold of his antlers and hang on for dear life. This time, as my strength waned, I temporarily lost my mind. I began to think my name was Jim Fowler. Remember him from Wild Kingdom, the assistant who was always getting attacked or chased by something? Out of the corner of my eye I could see the show's host, Marlin Perkins, smiling and making some kind of observation into my predicament. Then, just as I was beginning to wonder if my family had enough Mutual of Omaha coverage, I snapped back into reality, realizing that I had to again let go of Bambi's antlers to try to get away from him. When I did, Bambi, now a bloodthirsty beast intent on killing, turned from me and rammed Johnny Widener up against a chain link fence! An antler had penetrated Johnny's leg!

The situation was about to become critical when two more Fish and Wildlife employees rushed to the chain link fence from the other side and managed to tie off Bambi's antlers to the fence with a piece of rope.

The fight, which lasted nearly forty-five minutes, was finally over. Lauren came out of it unscathed. Johnny suffered cuts, bruises, and a nasty leg wound that required minor surgery. Clint Goins got most of the incident on tape without injury. In my case, I had no injuries, but I did feel so sore over the next few days that I felt as if a freight train had run over me. Bambi emerged from the brawl uninjured, victorious, and meaner than ever.

The great deer attack aired on *Kentucky Afield* in October of 1989, becoming the most popular segment in the show's forty-year history, according to audience response.

The Otter Project

In the spring of 1990, I found myself bound for the back country of southern Louisiana to videotape a river otter swap.

It was a trade that had been going on for years. A crew of biologists from the Kentucky Department of Fish and Wildlife would travel to the Louisiana swamps each year and purchase several dozen river otters from a Cajun trapper named Leroy Sevin (pronounced Sayvan). Then they would transport the otters to Missouri, where they were traded to that state for wild turkeys. Biologists then released the turkeys in Kentucky as part of an on-going restoration project. The reason Kentucky simply couldn't buy the turkeys from Missouri was because of a law that prohibits some states from accepting money for wildlife. But Missouri was more than willing to accept otters that it needed for its own restoration project.

This was to be one of the last runs to Louisiana as part of a wildlife trade. Kentucky's turkey population was growing stronger each year. Soon the restoration effort would be completed.

As we drove away that cold March morning I wondered what was in store for us. Would the mosquitoes down there really pick you up and carry you off? What about the alligators? Were the dark swamps of our destination really forbidden places rampant with black magic as some of the veterans of this annual journey had told me? I would find out soon enough.

The Wetlands of Louisiana

DAVE SHUFFETT'S OUTDOOR ADVENTURES

The leader of this expedition of sorts was Kentucky's Wild Turkey Coordinator, George Wright, a brilliant scientist with a booming voice and a country twang as thick as they come. George's team included Mark Cramer, a sharp-witted young biologist; Charlie Wilkins, a laid back biologist who loves to sing along to country music on the radio as he rolls down the highway; and Kentucky's Assistant State Wildlife Director, Ron Schureman, a tall white-haired man of German descent who claims he was nursed on beer instead of milk.

A day and a half after leaving Kentucky, we rolled into the bayou country of Louisiana, one of the most beautiful places I have ever seen. I'll never forget how green everything was. The swampy, coastal plain is a jungle of cypress, palmetto, and tall wetland grasses. And the swamps are a haven for animals: colorful egrets, songbirds, otters, swamp rabbits, and alligators, just to name a few. This is where we would find Leroy Sevin, a Cajun who had gained quite a bit of notoriety as the nation's premier otter supplier. Leroy live traps the otters back in the swamps and sells them to states in the business of otter restoration.

About twenty minutes outside Houma we pulled our caravan of trucks into a rock driveway leading up to a small, rustic house perched on the edge of a bayou. Near the house a short, white-haired man was standing over a huge black kettle. Ron Schureman, whom I had been riding with, commented, "It looks like Leroy is making supper for us again this year. Shuffett, you'll never forget this." I didn't know quite how to take Ron's comment. What was in that kettle?

Later that evening my fears were dispelled. Leroy and his wife, Diane, presented us a feast of shrimp, jambalaya, crab, and crawfish. After supper, Leroy told us stories of the swamps in a Cajun accent that was at times difficult to understand. I had become engrossed in his tales when, out of nowhere, Leroy turned to me and said, "Lukes lak its tahm fo you to hop in the peerow."

"Do what?" I asked.

George intervened and said with a smile on his face, "This is how we initiate any new folks who come here with us. You gotta' ride in it and try to keep it from tipping over. If you do tip it over, you could become alligator bait. Leroy says there's been a nine-foot 'gator in here at night."

"I've already been initiated into this agency once," I said, referring to the osprey trip.

"This is different," George replied in a firm voice. "This is your first trip to Leroy's place."

I began to wonder if each trip on this job would bring me a new initiation. These Fish and Wildlife people were the "initiatingist" bunch of folks I had ever known in my life. But had I refused to ride in the "peerow", whatever it was, I would have never heard the end of it.

When we walked outside and someone shined a flashlight on the "peerow", I was relieved. It looked a lot like a canoe to me. Leroy must have been reading my mind. "This ain't as easy as a canoe. You've got to stay steady," he said. (A "peerow", spelled *pirogue*, is a narrow boat for better maneuverability in swamps, a design that makes it easy to tip over.)

As soon as I put one foot in the boat, it became apparent just how unstable this thing was. The slightest jerk or twist of the body and over you go. But I managed to safely paddle away in the darkness, ever so rigid, as the Kentuckians and one Cajun laughingly wished me the best of luck. Almost immediately I thought of Sam, my golden retriever sidekick who usually travels with me.
"If not me, Sam would surely look like a tasty meal to a hungry 'gator. Thank goodness he's not along on this trip," I thought to myself.

Thirty minutes or so later I had become much more confident at piloting the pirogue. Gliding through the moonlit swamp, I began to think about the ecosystem around me: two hundred-year-old Cypress trees adorned with ghostly curtains of Spanish moss waving in the gentle night breeze and countless plant species emerging from the black water. I knew a thousand eyes were upon me because I could hear their voices, the creatures of the swamp.

Wetlands are one of the most important habitats because they house such a multitude of wildlife. Sadly enough, only a fraction of America's original wetlands remain. Most of them have been plowed under and converted to agricultural use or industrial development.

But this wetland was still here, withstanding the test of time. Eerie though it was in the dark of night, it was still a beautiful place to be.

Just as I was about to return to Leroy's house a sudden thrashing in the water behind my pirogue caused me to jump, and jerk my head around. The pirogue rocked from side to side! I was about to become alligator bait! Somehow I managed to steady up and keep from flipping over.
"Thank God," I said to myself. "That was a close call."

To this day I have no idea what made that noise in the water. It could have been any number of critters. It's probably best that I'll never know.

The next day, Leroy invited us to watch the feeding of his recently trapped otters. Several sheds surrounding Leroy's house were full of otters. When mealtime came, they let you know about it with a deafening half growl, half squeal.

Through trial and error, Leroy has found that ground nutria is the healthiest food for captive otters. (Nutria are large muskrat-like creatures of the swamps.)

The next morning we loaded eighty-eight otters into our trucks, and said good-bye to Leroy and Diane Sevin, two people who have dedicated their lives to the restoration of the river otter. We would now head north, skirt the Mississippi River, and turn left toward Missouri's heartland.

The otters may have taken the trip a lot better than some of us people. It was a long, tiring drive to Missouri.

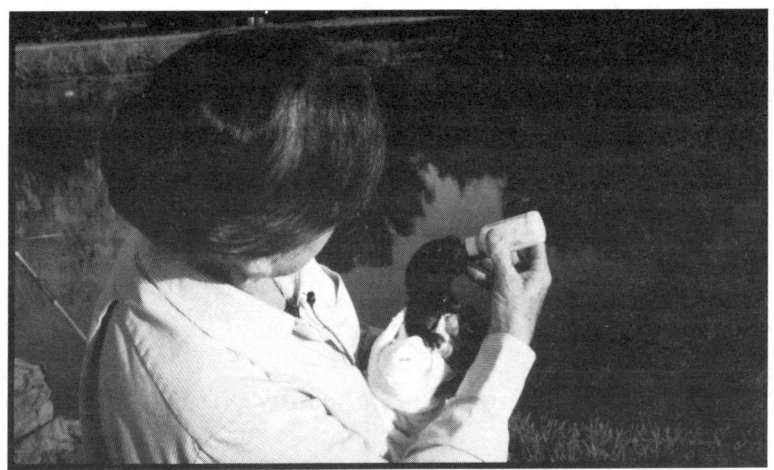

Baby Otter Being Fed by Diane Sevin

On this leg of the trip I rode with Charlie Wilkins, who made the journey a little easier for me. He's the one who loves to sing along to country music as he rolls down the "endless highway." Together we sang just about every country music chart buster that was ever written. In between songs, Charlie and I talked about the fate of the river otters.

He told me that the otter is a hardy, adaptable animal that would do well in Missouri despite the change in habitat and climate.

Originally, river otters were common across the United States and Canada, but loss of wetland habitat, pollution, and unregulated trapping decades ago caused their numbers to decline dramatically.

Today, thanks to scientific wildlife management, regulated harvest, and the protection of the species in many states, the otter is making a slow recovery.

Twenty hours or so after leaving Louisiana we made it to Columbia, Missouri, where an assembly of Missouri Department of Conservation scientists took the otters off our hands.

The next day, eighty-eight healthy otters were released in various streams and wetlands across Missouri.

The otter trip aired on *Kentucky Afield* in the spring of 1990. Two years later, Kentucky began its own successful river otter restoration program.

Days with the Governor

By the summer of 1992 I had been involved in otter, osprey, bald eagle, and black bear projects, and I had hunted and fished with dozens upon dozens of fine sportsmen.

Speaking of hunting and fishing, by now I was getting many invitations from good-hearted sportsmen who wanted to share their expertise with me. These folks had seen too many shows in which I had bombed out on the water or had left the field without any game. One such concerned viewer was the last person I expected to hear from: Kentucky Governor Wallace Wilkinson. On his first contact, he said, "Shuffett, you're a fine outdoor TV show host, but you can't ever seem to catch a decent fish. I'd love to come on your program and show you how it's done."

"Of course, Governor," I nervously replied. "I need all the help I can get."

In early July the governor and a few of his aides, along with Fish and Wildlife Commissioner Don McCormick, assistant producer Scott Mullins, and me, headed off to Lake Barkley in western Kentucky, where we'd heard the white bass were jumping.

Just before we loaded up a couple of boats with fishing gear, TV equipment, and people, the governor jokingly said, "Shuffett, I can't believe you get paid for doing this kind of thing. I'll be going out of office at the end of the year. You think you might need an assistant producer?"

"Governor, we could sure use some additional help," I replied. "But I don't know if I could pay you very much."

"That's O.K.," said the governor. "Being unemployed, I'll take what I can get. Besides, you'll give me a raise after the first year because I'm gonna' teach you how to hunt and fish. Lord knows somebody's gonna' have to."

The governor was surprised to find out that I could catch a fish every now and then, at least in the jumps. Using white spoons, we caught one white bass after another for several hours.

Dave Fishing with Governor Wallace Wilkinson

Later in the day, we headed to the Ballard Wildlife Management Area near the Mississippi River in far western Kentucky, where the governor joined us on a jon-boat excursion through the dense cypress and tupelo swamps that area is known for. We slowly wound our way through an ancient forest on water. All the while, a majestic bald eagle circled the sky just above the cypress canopy. Within the forest, near at hand, a red-headed woodpecker hammered away at a standing snag and a great blue heron stood on a cypress knee cautiously tolerating our intrusion, watching our every move. The governor was overwhelmed by the surroundings.

"Never have I seen anyplace more beautiful," he said.

In my opinion, to truly appreciate a wetland you have to see it the way the governor did, by boat, close enough to touch the cypress trees, close enough to bask in all its splendor.

A couple of months later I was sitting at home early one Saturday morning looking out the window at a beautiful sunrise when the phone rang. I presumed it was my father, who usually calls early on Saturdays, but when I picked up the phone it wasn't him.

The voice on the other end said, "Dave, how the hell are you? This is the governor."

Shocked that a governor would call me at home on a Saturday morning, I spilled a full cup of coffee in my lap. Grimacing with pain I replied, "Doing just fine, Governor. Just having a cup of coffee."

"I've been noticing your hunting and fishing hasn't improved that much since the last time we were together," the governor remarked. "But I wanted to tell you that the time I had with y'all down there in western Kentucky was one of the most enjoyable days I've had in my life. And if you ever take a notion you want to do another show with me, I'd be honored."

We did one more show with Wallace Wilkinson before he went out of office. This time we took him to the other end of Kentucky, Cumberland Mountain near the Virginia border, a place just as grand as the wetlands more than four hundred miles to the west. On a beautiful autumn afternoon we made our way up the mountain to Shillalah Creek, a pristine, boulder-laden stream known for its brook trout. Shillalah Creek is a rare jewel. Not many streams in the southeastern United States are clean enough to support brook trout, a species that can't tolerate pollution.

Using ultra-light gear and small spinners, we fished eddies and quiet pools. On this day the fish refused to cooperate. But at least the governor didn't give me too hard a time, since he wasn't catching any fish either.

Fortunately, Fisheries Biologist Doug Stephens was on hand to give the show a new focus: his backpack shocker, a device used to study fish populations. It is basically a generator that can be strapped to one's back. A cord and a long electrode extend out from the generator, which allows Doug to wade in a stream, immersing the electrode in the water in front of him, shocking any fish in the proximity. The fish rise to the surface, temporarily stunned but unharmed.

Doug waded one of the pools where we had been fishing, and to my surprise, shocked up several fish. At least the governor was able to see what a brook trout looks like. Meanwhile, I sat on a nearby boulder scratching my head, wondering why those fish wouldn't bite. In this moment of despair I thought of a saying unlucky fishermen have used time and time again to make themselves feel better. "If you caught a fish every time you threw a line in the water it wouldn't be fun anymore."

As the sun dropped below the mountain tops the governor and his entourage said good-bye and climbed into a caravan of vehicles.
Before he drove away the governor smiled and said, "Remember, Dave, I'll soon be unemployed. Keep me in mind."
Of course, the governor never sent me his resume, but I'll have to say that his quick wit, his perennial sense of humor, and his love for hunting, fishing, and the outdoors would qualify him as a pretty good outdoor television host. Maybe, for my sake, I should be glad he never tried to get on board.

The Confidence Factor

Even though the governor was merely making jokes about my hunting and fishing abilities, or lack thereof, there was and still is an element of truth in his remarks. Admittedly, I am not the expert sportsman who always gets a trophy deer or a wall hanging fish. But when someone who is not that good to begin with, such as myself, begins to lose confidence, you're talking about a dry spell -- and I mean a dry spell. For a period of about a year it seemed that if I had any luck at all, it was bad. On fishing segments I spent most of my time untangling line or retrieving lures from tree branches while the guests on the show caught all the fish. On hunting segments I was missing my target ninety percent of the time. I remember an on-camera comment outdoor writer Norm Minch made while we were videotaping a rabbit hunting segment. "As usual, Dave shot two or three times and missed the rabbit. The rabbit ran toward me, and, naturally, I took the opportunity to shoot him. Thanks, Dave, for your continued support."

A Rabbit Hunting Shot (taken from video)

Things began to change for me during the videotaping of another rabbit hunting feature. Friend and avid small game hunter Bobby Reese was one of the guests on that particular show. Bobby made the following statement to me on camera.

"Dave, I've seen you miss so often that I'm willing to bet you five dollars that you won't get a rabbit while we're out here today."

"O.K. Bobby, I'll take you up on that," I reluctantly replied. Two hours later I was beginning to wonder if it was going to be another, yes another, one of those days. But just as all hope was fading, two of Bobby's beagle hounds jumped a rabbit out of a nearby thicket. I quickly raised my shotgun to my shoulder, aimed at the bolting rabbit as it crossed in front of me, and followed through, much like a golfer does when he strikes a golf ball. That rabbit made it to the dinner table and I made five dollars. More importantly, I regained some of that lost confidence. Of course, Bobby looked at it differently. "Even a blind hog can find an acorn every now and then," he said.

The dictionary defines confidence as a feeling of certainty, self-reliance, and boldness. When these emotions are rushing through your veins, it can make all the difference in the world. As in hunting, if you know you're going to catch a fish, you're much more likely to do so. Your casting and bait presentation is much better on days when your confidence level is high. Perhaps there really is a mysterious aura around people who are confident. Fish just want to bite their lures and no one else's.

That aura must have been surrounding me one hot afternoon in May of 1992. We were videotaping a farm pond fishing segment near my home in southern Kentucky. The guests on that show included my father, my sister, Marilynn, and my brother, Bill. Our angle was the promotion of fishing as a fun, healthy, family activity. It was one of those days when everything worked well. The message I had hoped for was coming across loud and clear.

Commenting on camera my father said, "It's mind boggling what's going on in the world today. If families would spend more time doing what we're doing today the world would be a lot better off."

"Too many kids today aren't exposed to this kind of activity," my sister said. "They're spending way too much time in front of the TV set. And they'll never have the wonderful memories of the outdoors like we do."

My brother remarked, "Farm ponds, rivers and streams are all over this part of the country. You don't need an expensive bass boat and all that fancy equipment. I've done my share of fishing on the major impoundments, and they're a lot of fun. But what we're doing today is still my favorite."

After the on-camera commentary we concentrated a little more on catching fish. Using small spinners, small crankbaits, and live worms, we hooked into plenty of bluegill and small bass. "But why not try for the biggest largemouth bass in that pond?" I asked myself. So, I opened up my tackle box and grabbed a huge, yellow spinner bait made by the Grim Reaper Company. That thing was enormous. In fact, I had used it as a muskie bait just a few weeks earlier. As I tied it on a bass rig with 14-pound test line, videographer Scott Mullins said, "If you do catch a fish, he's gonna' be a monster." My confidence level was high, and if there is such a thing as an aura it was all around me.

"Of course he's gonna' be a monster," I replied. "And I'm gonna' catch him right over there by that structure within two casts." On the second cast he hit it with a mighty jolt that took my breath away. "Fish on!" I shouted. My rod doubled over and the drag began to pull. I remember hearing my dad shouting instructions to me, as if I were eight years old all over again, "Hang on to him Dave! Let him run with it!" Then he broke the water making himself visible for the first time. It is hard to put into words the multitude of emotions I was feeling at that moment. Ecstatic, anxious, and prayerful are a few words that come to mind. After battling that fish for several minutes I managed to get him to the bank. What a prize! None of us had scales on hand but we guessed him to weigh between six and seven pounds.

The Big One that Didn't Get Away!

Most of the time I'm a catch and release fisherman. But I had that bass mounted because it was the only time in my life I told the person next to me that I was going to catch a big bass at the precise time I caught him. In other words, I called the shot. Whatever it was -- pure luck, confidence, or divine intervention -- it will probably never happen again.

Timeless Tom Kelly

That was a nice largemouth I pulled out of that farm pond, but not quite as big as an eight-pounder caught by retired farmer Tom Kelly. Tom landed his lunker at another Kentucky pond in 1991. What's so great about another big bass caught out of a pond? In 1991, when he caught that fish, Tom Kelly was 103 years old. He's now 105 and still fishing. Possibly the oldest active sportsman in America, Tom, or "Pop," as he's affectionately called, has taken time to go fishing every day, weather permitting, for one hundred years.

My travels while producing an outdoor show have taken me west to Texas and Utah, across the Southeast, and down just about every path in Kentucky. But none of those great experiences can top one day I had in 1992 fishing a farm pond with Tom Kelly.

We caught up with Tom on a warm spring morning at his home near Stamping Ground, Kentucky, a tiny community named for the ancient Buffalo herds that once trampled the area. There he was sitting on the back porch of the family farmhouse with fishing gear in hand, obviously eager to go fishing.

When I introduced myself to Tom, he said in a soft spoken voice slightly slurred with age, "Nice to meet you. My youngest boy would like to go fishing with us, if that's O.K. with you."

105 Year-old Tom Kelly -- Possibly America's Oldest Active Sportsman

"Sure," I replied. "Bring him along." So, seventy-five-year-old Clyde and his wife, Iva, joined us for a day of fishing.

As we headed down the road to a neighboring farm pond I thought of dozens of questions I wanted to ask Tom. After all, when he threw his first line in the water at the age of five, the Civil War was still fresh on people's minds. The Indian Wars of the American West were just winding down, and Grover Cleveland had just moved into the White House for the second time. What was it like to be alive in those days? What does he think of the world today?

A five or six-mile drive down a winding two-lane road had taken us to one of Tom's favorite ponds. As we walked to the pond I noticed how spry Tom was. He could get around almost as well as the rest of us. While Tom rigged up a couple of fishing poles with worms and floaters, I spent a few minutes talking with Clyde and Iva. Thinking Tom must have always eaten just the right foods, low fat, low cholesterol, and possibly a lot of salad, I asked Iva about his diet. Her answer was shocking, and I might add, encouraging, at least for me. "He's always eaten a lot of greasy food," she told me. "He just loves anything greasy. Every morning I fix him sausage and eggs, and he's got to have his molasses, even over a slice of pie. At supper time Pop likes about anything fried." Iva went on to tell me that Tom will even eat the hunk of fat cooked with a pot of beans.

Tom should write a book about his lifelong diet. It would certainly stand out among all those other diet and nutrition books on the shelves today!

"He's also chewed a lot of tobacco," Clyde said. "That don't have anything to do with eatin', but he's been doing it now on a hundred years." I told Clyde that as soon as we finished fishing I would head to the nearest country store and buy myself some chewing tobacco. Who knows, maybe that's the secret to longevity!

I asked Clyde what it was like, at the age of seventy-five, to go fishing every day with his dad. "It's wonderful," he said. "I'm an awful lucky fella', but the bad thing about it is, he's still the boss."

Tom had settled down in a lawn chair and had already caught a bluegill when I began talking with him. As Scott Mullins rolled the camera, I asked the obvious first question.
"Mr. Kelly, what do you attribute your long life to?"
"I don't know," he said with a handful of tobacco in his mouth.
Now I was really beginning to suspect that chewing tobacco had something to do with long life.

Tom went on to tell me about his century-long love affair with fishing.
"When I was a boy I'd go fishin' down at Elkhorn Creek. We didn't have none of them fancy reels and poles. I'd cut off a sycamore limb and tie a string to it."

At that point Clyde walked over to us, winked at me, and asked his father a question that has been asked of dads for countless generations.

"What am I doin' wrong, Pop? I can't get 'em to bite."

"I can't either, son. I guess we just ain't holdin' our mouths right," Tom replied.

Tom began to recall more images of his life around the turn of the century.

"Most of the time we got around on horses. My uncle would bring back wild horses from out west and I'd break 'em." (Tom was raised by an uncle who was a veteran of the Confederacy.)

"I did buy a Model-T once," Tom went on to say. "I paid twelve dollars for it. I didn't have much use for it, though. So, I ended up givin' it to my boys."

Tom's floater suddenly disappeared under the water. With the agility of a much younger man, Tom jerked his rod back to set the hook. With a twinkle in those ancient eyes and a smile on his face, he played the fish for a minute or so, then lifted a keeper largemouth bass out of the water. I could tell that in Tom Kelly's mind, this was what life was all about. The joy of catching a fish: no less triumphant a moment than the day he caught his first one a hundred years ago.

As he baited his hook with another worm, I asked Tom what he thought of life around the turn of the century as compared to now.

"Some things have got better, some worse," he said. "Young folks don't know right from wrong like they used to. And there's a lot more killin' going on these days."

"Do we need to go back to some of those old-fashioned values?" I asked.

"Yeah, we do," he said.

Many people today would disagree with Tom. They would say the traditions and values of yesteryear are antiquated and have no place in modern society. "Who can define what is right and what is wrong?" some would go so far as to ask. Those people need to take a long, hard look at national statistics. Violence in schools is reaching an all-time high. Kids are killing other kids over pairs of sneakers, and in some cases simply because they wanted to kill somebody. A nation once united is now splitting into special interest factions and hate groups. Those old-fashioned values Tom Kelly was referring to may not be so bad after all. I hope, and believe, that one day our country will return to the values that he knew.

As midday approached we loaded up our TV equipment and fishing gear, and said good-bye to the Kelly family. Tom told me that he planned to keep on fishing in the years ahead. "I want to catch me a nine-pound bass," he said.

For me it was an experience I'll never forget, for I had looked into the eyes of a man who had seen the 19th century. On the wings of his memory I went on a journey through time, back to the days of horse-drawn carriages and sycamore fishing poles.

The Bear Project

The leaves were at their most spectacular, blazing of red, gold, and everything in between. It was a beautiful time to be in the Great Smoky Mountains National Park.

We were there to videotape *Ursus americanus*, the black bear. Bears have been moving into the mountains of eastern Kentucky for a decade or so. They're on a natural range expansion from North Carolina, Tennessee, Virginia and West Virginia. But their numbers in Kentucky are still relatively low, and we had been struggling to get Kentucky bears on tape for quite some time. Our solution to that problem was simple. We would travel to the Smokies, where bears are much more common, do our show from there, and tie it all back into Kentucky.

Kentucky Wildlife Biologist Larry Short, an authority on black bears, and his assistant, Herbie Adams, joined me on the trek into the Smokies, along with David Gibson and Scott Mullins of the television staff.

The National Park Service people told us bears had been seen at the base of Mount LaConte frequently. So we headed into the wilderness with high hopes. As we hiked through some of the wildest country in the eastern United States Larry told us about problems with bear and human encounters.

"A lot of people tend to forget these are wild animals," he said. "They appear docile and cumbersome, to the point of being cuddly. People want to get close to the bears, feed them, and pet them. This is inviting disaster. They have incredibly fast reflexes and can sprint up to thirty-five miles per hour."

Later, a Park Ranger would tell us a horror story about a tourist who tried to set his child on the back of an adult black bear. Fortunately, the bear chose to run away from the obtrusive humans rather than attack. But it could have been a tragedy.

"The few bear attacks that occur are usually unintentionally instigated by humans," Larry said. "If people would respect their space by staying back a considerable distance and never offer them food, bear attacks would be even more infrequent. And people who live in black bear country should keep household garbage in containers with lids and consider putting electric fences around gardens and bee hives. These measures would greatly reduce bear problems," he said.

A day and a half of hiking along the lower slopes of Mt. LaConte had turned up nothing when, finally, Larry spotted the first bear sign, claw marks on a tree. Within a few yards of there Larry spotted a decaying fallen tree that had been ripped open sometime during the last couple of days. A bear had torn it apart looking for grubs. Then, David Gibson nearly stepped in fresh bear droppings. We now knew a bear was close at hand, and there was a good chance *Ursus americanus* was watching our every move.

"I can tell you boys are getting uneasy," Larry whispered.

"I'd rather have 'em with that attitude than wanting to go up and pet one," Herbie said.

"Just remember, keep your distance as much as possible," Larry said. "I know you boys want to get decent footage, but if you do get those cameras too close the bear may run off or do just the opposite and charge. If he does come at you, there's a good chance it will be a bluff charge." (Black bears are noted for bluff charging, running at full force toward a threatening presence, usually a human, then coming to a grinding halt, sometimes just inches away from the unwelcome visitor.)

"You just gotta' stand your ground," Larry said.

"You mean I gotta' stand there while a bear comes at me full force?" Scott asked.

"That's right," Larry replied. "You sure as hell can't outrun them and it won't do you any good to climb a tree, but if you stand your ground they're more than likely gonna' bluff and back off. Then, all you have to deal with is a pair of wet trousers."

"How can folks avoid getting into that situation?" I asked.

"It's just like we talked about before," Larry replied. "Don't purposely get too close to a bear and make him feel backed against a wall, so to speak. On the other hand, sometimes people can walk up on a bear if it's a windy day. Bears want to keep their distance from humans, unless they're used to being fed. But sometimes, wind can prevent bears from detecting the presence of humans through hearing and smell. To avoid that possibility, hikers should talk to one another and not try to sneak through the woods. Lone hikers might even consider singing to themselves, whistling, or possibly wearing bells on their backpack."

Larry had just pointed out another clawed tree when Scott shouted in a whisper, "I've got one! I've got one!" At first the rest of us couldn't see what Scott was looking at that caused him to get so excited. Then, with our eyes straining, we saw a black spot some distance away ambling through dense undergrowth. This was the moment we had been anxiously awaiting. We moved in somewhat closer for videotaping purposes, but not too close.

"It's a sow with two cubs," Herbie whispered.

At this point our hearts were pounding with excitement. Scott and David began rolling their cameras, taking advantage of powerful zoom lenses. For an hour or so the bears never acknowledged our presence. Perhaps they knew we were there but we weren't close enough to intimidate them.

<u>Ursus americanus</u> -- The Black Bear

As is the case with most young creatures, humans included, the cubs were made of energy, boundless energy. They climbed trees, swam in a nearby stream and bounced and rolled in circles around the sow, never giving her a minute's peace. Once she tried to lie down, but the cubs saw it as a golden opportunity to playfully maul her. She didn't try to stop them. It was as if she were either enjoying it, or so tired she couldn't muster the energy to do much about it.

For this brief moment in time everything was right. The bears were at peace in a wilderness of tall oaks, hemlocks, and pristine mountain streams. But how long would it last? How long can these creatures co-exist with millions of tourists who converge on the park in growing numbers every year? And what is the future of all bears in North America? Bears require vast expanses of wilderness range. As we humans continue our relentless encroachment, our ceaseless development of ranch land, houses, highways, and tall shiny buildings, and our final push into the last remnant wilds of North America, I wonder if the family *Ursidae* has any chance at all.

Scott and David had rolled tape for the better part of an hour when the sow caught wind of us and hurried her cubs up the mountain out of sight. That was the last we saw of them.

7

Technical Difficulties

Black bear sign was a major component of our bear show. We wanted to show the viewer what to look for. We had discovered a bear trail, a log ripped apart, several trees with claw marks, and fresh droppings.

We were particularly excited about the droppings because Larry, upon close examination, could determine what the bear had been eating. The viewer would not only learn what bear droppings look like, but what the omnivore had for lunch as well.

All of us were a little worried about audience response to this close-up shot that would fill up a TV screen. On the other hand, how could we point out all the other bear sign and leave out the aftereffects of an important bodily function that happens to the bear several times a day?

The decision was made to roll tape. David Gibson crouched down with the camera and rolled on a close-up while Larry stirred around the stuff with a twig, finding enough composure to explain what he was seeing to the viewer.

On the way back to Kentucky, we talked of how well things had gone for us in the Smokies. Larry and Herbie had performed superbly in front of the camera. The folks at the National Park Service had gone out of their way to help us, the weather cooperated, and we found bears. A good show was in the making.

I am a firm believer in rewinding the tape and reviewing what has been shot while we're out on location. It is simply a matter of taking a few minutes to look through the viewfinder and listen through earphones as the tape rewinds to make sure everything is there.

As we unloaded the gear back at our studios in Frankfort, Kentucky, I realized we had forgotten to look at one of the tapes back in the Smokies. It's one of those things that makes a television producer cringe.

You might know the tape we didn't review was the one with the bear droppings on it. As it turned out, that whole sequence was unusable because of glitches (tears) on the tape. What bum luck!

Scott Mullins and I sat in front of the television monitor puzzled as to how to recover from this unfortunate situation.

"Ah-ha, I think I've got the answer," I told Scott. "We've got bears on display here at the complex."

"I think I know where you're going with this," Scott said. "You want to drop in a shot of bear poop from here."

"That's right," I said. "It's a little deceptive, but at least the viewer who's unfamiliar with bear sign will get to see a close-up of what it looks like."

I approached animal caretaker Johnny Widener, the fellow who had unsuccessfully tried to rescue us from the great deer attack a few years earlier.

"Johnny, I've got a big favor to ask of you. I need to borrow some bear droppings from the display area."

"You need what?" Johnny asked.

"It's a long story," I replied. "We need to videotape it for a black bear segment we're doing."

With a puzzled look on his face Johnny said, "You don't have to tell me any more. I learned a long time ago that if I ask you TV fellows too many questions I just get more confused."

Johnny proceeded to enter the bear enclosure with shovel in hand.

"Any particular size, shape, or condition you want it in?" Johnny asked.

"Beggars can't be choosers. But if you can find anything reasonably fresh we'd certainly appreciate it," I said.

Johnny handed me a shovel-full of fresh droppings that Scott and I drove to a nearby wooded area and placed on the ground. Scott rolled on a close-up, the same as David Gibson had done back in the Smokies. When the show aired, the audience saw a quick three-second close-up shot of droppings that had come from a different bear, far away from the Great Smoky Mountains National Park.

The bear poop incident is an example of the difficulties associated with producing a weekly outdoor television show. Seldom does all that complex machinery we carry with us out in the elements work perfectly. Other problems are created by nature herself. Extreme cold and heat are not insurmountable hurdles. In fact, those of us who spend a great deal of our lives outside have adapted somewhat to extreme temperatures. The equipment also handles them well. But shut downs and cancellations because of heavy rains are quite common. Television equipment and rain don't mix well. And there are days when the weather is perfect but the game is nowhere to be found, or the fish won't bite. One common line we hear on location is, "If only you boys had been here just yesterday. The fish were biting like crazy." Often the guests on the show who have invited us to their favorite fishing hole tend to blame themselves for nature's mysterious ways. "I don't know what's wrong with 'em, boys. I'm sure sorry about this," they tell us in a remorseful tone. I always remind those folks of what they already know. You can't always predict what the fish or game are going to do. That's what makes hunting and fishing such a challenge.

Those less than perfect days are anticipated. We know that some shoots will have to be rescheduled or that we'll have to stay on location for an extra day or two until the fish finally decide to bite again. As for the perception of the viewing audience, it may often look as if we went out for half an hour or so and caught one fish after another, when in actuality the shoot may have taken a couple of days to complete.

And then there are the totally unexpected events, one of which took place back home on Green River. Former University of Kentucky basketball coach Joe B. Hall, an ardent stream fisherman, and Fish and Wildlife Commissioner Don McCormick accepted my invitation to float a twelve mile stretch of the river. As talked about in the first chapter of this book I had spent much of my boyhood days on the Green, but living away from home for many years had made it difficult for me to remember the characteristics of that stretch of river and where all the productive holes were. So, I asked local Conservation Officer and Green River fisherman Todd Rogers to give us a hand by acting as our guide. Todd was more than willing to help and excited that two men of such stature, the Fish and Wildlife Commissioner and a legendary basketball coach, were planning to fish his river.

When we rendezvoused at the river bank on that hot summer morning we noticed Todd was sweating profusely, much more than anyone else.

"Are you feeling all right?" I asked.

"It must have been something I ate. I'm a little sick at my stomach, but I'll be fine," Todd replied.

"Are you sure?" Commissioner McCormick asked.

"Yes sir. Don't y'all worry about me. I'll get better as the day goes on," Todd assured us all.

Coach Joe B. Hall, Dave, and Commissioner Don McCormick Fishing on Green River

Joe Hall, Commissioner McCormick, and I climbed into one boat while Todd and videographers Alfred Fields and Scott Mullins loaded themselves and camera gear into another. We headed downstream side by side.

As much as Todd wanted to get better, he didn't. Four miles or so into the trip he turned white as a ghost, and every few minutes he was becoming violently sick at his stomach, a scene that made for a most unusual fishing trip for all involved.

To our amazement, Todd refused to give in to whatever was plaguing him.

"I'm all right," he told us again as he lay down in his boat.

"No he's not all right. We need to get him out of the game," Joe Hall whispered.

Commissioner McCormick and I agreed. We decided to cut the trip short. But Todd would have nothing to do with that.

"I know a place I can get out just a little ways downstream and call someone on my radio to come get me. That way y'all can go on. That's what I want," he told us.

All of us wondered if a person that sick should be allowed to have any choices, but we reluctantly let him do what he wanted. Todd slowly made his way up the wooded river bank and out of sight, leaving Alfred and Scott to paddle his boat on downstream.

It wasn't a great fishing day. We caught a few small bass, and Coach Hall hooked one channel catfish. But all things considered, we weren't upset at all. The river was in less than good condition, as was our guide, who all but died along the way. We found out that Todd had contracted a severe stomach virus that took him several days to get over. "I don't think I've ever felt that sick in all my life," he later told me.

Never in my career as a television producer has someone gone that far above and beyond the call of duty to help me get a show done. Todd Rogers was determined to fulfill his commitment to guide us downstream, battling his sickness like a courageous warrior, and like a scene from an old movie, the wounded soldier asked to be left behind when he couldn't go on any longer, so the noble mission could be carried out unhindered.

Todd Rogers' untimely illness was another example of the many unplanned script changes that come about when producing a weekly outdoor show. Todd apologized for his ailment repeatedly, as if he could have done something about it. I had to remind him of what he already knew. "You can't predict when you're going to get sick, and there's absolutely nothing to feel guilty about. It's just one of those unforeseen hurdles," I told him.

The unexpected is a fact of life for outdoor television producers. But our lives are rich with memories of happy endings, for no matter what the outcome of our weekly exploits, just being out there witnessing the awe-inspiring grandeur of nature unfold before our eyes is a blessing unto itself.

8

Tall Tales

On those less than perfect days that have been hampered with bad luck or rain, some idle time usually ensues as the TV crew and the guests sit around and wait for the rain to stop, or the fish or game to cooperate again. And when there is idle time sportsmen will inevitably begin to recall their favorite hunting and fishing tales. I have spent many an hour engrossed in a yarn that may be partially true, greatly exaggerated, or purely invented.

Not long ago I spent some time with sixty-two year-old Z.T. Lester, a Kentuckian who has devoted a great deal of his life to quail hunting. Z.T. told me a story about a fellow he called Grandpap.

"My father-in-law and I went hunting one year in Adair County. We were looking for a special place to hunt. After searching for awhile, we found a farm that looked like a good place for quail to feed and hide. We pulled up to a farmhouse driveway, walked up to the front door of the house, and asked the landowner for permission to hunt on the farm. The landowner granted us permission and told us that we didn't need to use our bird dogs. We asked him how in the world we'd find quail without dogs. He said we could use his grandfather to find the birds. Since the landowner had been kind enough to give us permission to hunt on his place, we didn't argue about it. So, we left our dogs in the cage, and Grandpap took off with us. And believe it or not, he started finding birds. He would even point single birds for us. What a delightful day of hunting we had! We filled our bags with quail and thanked Grandpap for one of the greatest hunting days of our lives. We asked him if we could come back next season, and he said that would be fine.

"On the first day of hunting season a year later, we went back to the same farm in Adair county, leaving our dogs at home. We pulled up to the farmer's house to again request permission to hunt and, most of all, to use Grandpap. The farmer told us we could hunt on his property, but we couldn't use Grandpap. We asked him why we couldn't use him. After all, he was so much better at finding quail than our dogs. The farmer paused, then with a sympathetic tone told us his Grandpap was gone. We asked what happened. The farmer then told us the whole tragic story. He said, 'Near the end of last bird season we took Grandpap to hunt quail and he started running rabbits. We had to shoot him. Poor old Grandpap.' "

Z.T. told me another story about a dog he used to have that never made a false point.

"Early one morning I was taking some visiting friends on a hunting trip. My dog, old Jack, was in the back seat. We were riding along and all of a sudden Jack went into a point. I said, 'We'd better stop the car. There must be a covey of birds nearby, and old Jack never false points.' We pulled the car over to the side of the road, got out, loaded our guns, and were preparing for the big shoot. Old Jack was still on a point inside the car. There was a man standing on the road near where we were. I walked up to him and asked him who owned the land we were wanting to hunt. 'I do,' he said. We told him about old Jack making the point and asked him if we could hunt around there to try to find the birds. He said we could, and we looked and looked and looked, but there were no quail to be found. I was puzzled because Jack had never lied before. I said, 'Fellows, I don't know what's the matter, but I guess old Jack must have told his first lie.' We made our way back to the car, where the landowner was still standing. We thanked him for allowing us to hunt on his place. I asked, 'Sir, could I please get your name before we go? We may want to hunt here again.' 'Sure,' he said. 'My name is Bob White.' I said, 'See fellows, I told you old Jack never lies.' "

When I first began producing outdoor television I needed all the help I could get, not to say I still don't. But what I really needed then was the advice of a veteran sportsman with years of experience in the field (quite literally), and in the field of communicating stories of the outdoors to the public.

In the first few weeks of my new position I had the good fortune of meeting a fellow who had both of those skills, outdoor writer and former television director Ben Hall. Ben was graciously willing to take the time to share a lifetime of experience with a greenhorn kid.

Dave's Mentor, Ben Hall, Giving Dave Some Advice

Since we became friends in 1989 Ben and I have hunted and fished together, solved the problems of the world, and told a tall tale or two to each other. He recently shared an old tale with me that's not one of his originals, but one of his favorites.

"Several years ago, my cousin Ed decided that he ought to get into deer hunting. Since we agreed that he ought to learn from a master, I naturally agreed to take him myself.

"I'd decided that we would go down to Todd County, which is where I grew up, and hunt on a place owned by an uncle of mine, who was then in his eighties. I'd hunted there many times and knew pretty well where the good bucks could be found.

"Ed and his new Marlin 30-30 arrived the day before the season opened and we decided to drive over to Todd County to look over the place we were going to hunt the next morning.

"It was one of those warm November afternoons and Ed had just finished a long, boring drive from Louisville to my place. So, on the way to Todd County, he fell asleep.

"When we arrived at Uncle Pearly's place, Ed was still sleeping, so I decided not to wake him. He would have plenty of time to meet the old gentleman later on.

"My uncle was as kind as ever and said that he would be glad for us to hunt his farm anytime we wanted to. Then he added, 'If it's not too much trouble, I wish you'd do something for me. It's something I just can't bring myself to do.' Tears came to the old fellow's eyes as he was talking.

"He had kept a pair of good mules for years, long after most everybody else had given up using animal power, and long after the animals were too old to do any work anyway.

"Ida, the mare mule, had passed quietly away some time before and now Dan was suffering the infirmities of old age. I had seen him standing in the field near the long, gravel lane that led to the house when we came in and he seemed to be on his last legs.

"Uncle Pearly wanted me to put the aged animal out of his misery; he and his sons just couldn't bring themselves to do what needed to be done for the faithful family servant.

"Naturally, I had to agree to the old man's request, as little as it appealed to me. A short time later, I left Uncle Pearly sitting by his fire and headed back to the truck where Ed was still sleeping.

"About the time I stepped off the porch, an evil influence overcame me. If I was going to have to carry out the onerous task with the old mule, at least I could try to make the most of the opportunity to put one over on Ed.

"He woke up when I slammed the truck door as hard as I could and headed the vehicle for the road.

" 'I can't believe that old man,' I said, sounding as exasperated and angry as I could. 'My own uncle and he's decided that he won't let anybody, even us, hunt on his place anymore. And after all the favors I've done for him.'

"Ed didn't say anything but 'Hmmm.'

"We were heading down the lane and old Dan was standing just where I had last seen him. I slammed on the brakes and slid the truck to a stop in a cloud of dust.

" 'I'll teach that old man a lesson,' I growled. 'If he won't let us hunt here, one good turn deserves another.' I yanked the .30-06 from the rack in the back window of the cab, bolted a round into the chamber, and rested the rifle on the half-raised glass in the window.

"Just before I pulled the trigger, I thought I heard Ed rolling down his window and I figured he was about to be sick.

"One shot allowed the elderly mule to join his friend Ida in greener pastures. As I was clearing the rifle and waiting for Ed's reaction, I heard three quick shots go off behind me as Ed worked the lever on his new 30-30 that he had poked out the other window.

" 'All right, all right,' he yelled happily. 'We'll show him. I just shot three of his cows.' "

When Ben finished telling me that story he assured me it wasn't true, as if I needed convincing. He said he first heard a version of it back in the 1940's in a traveling tent show. Since then, everybody under the sun has told a version of that tale, from himself to comedian Jerry Clower.

Alfred Fields, an assistant producer on my staff, is quite a comedian and storyteller in his own right.

Alfred comes from the mountains of eastern Kentucky, where ruffed grouse hunting is a popular pastime. He once told me a story about three kinds of bird dogs.

" 'Some bird dogs look so much alike you can't tell them apart; however, after hunting with every conceivable breed, my hunting buddies and I have determined there are several types of bird dogs. If you've ever hunted ruffed grouse with a dog, you'll recognize these three: 'You Go First,' 'See You in the Next County,' and 'Mr. Perfection.'

" 'You Go First' proves appearances are deceiving. After only a short time in the woods, this type bird dog loses interest in searching for the prized game bird. He's content to sniff our heels and act bored. Every attempt to throw him in the brush, hoping he'll realize what's required of him, only adds to our frustration as he returns with tail tucked between his legs. No amount of coaxing, screaming or crying will move him from under our feet. Finally, against all odds, we shoot and a bird falls. The command, 'fetch,' however, has vanished from the dog's memory.

"Now, 'See You in the Next County' is just the opposite. When the dog box is opened on hunting day, this type bird dog is transformed into a clawing Tasmanian devil as he crashes through the door and disappears in the distance. Yelling and screaming, we frantically search for our whistles. (But we may as well have left them home.) Right away we realize the dog's pointing instinct must have been left in the dog box because we see bird after bird flush from the direction 'See You in the Next County' was last observed. And if we're lucky enough to take a bird, the dog keeps his ability to retrieve a secret. He only appears for a fleeting moment to check out the noise of the gun before disappearing again in the distance.

Mr. Perfection (a.k.a. "Doc")

"Finally, 'Mr. Perfection' is the type of bird dog every hunter dreams of. After releasing him from the dog box, this dog waits patiently while we get our guns from the truck, don and fill our hunting vests with shells and take several minutes to decide which direction we'll take. Once we're ready, 'Mr. Perfection' hunts every conceivable place a bird could be hiding. With only a wave of his master's hand, he immediately goes in the direction indicated. He smells every bird in the woods and approaches with great caution. He locks into a beautiful point and remains motionless as the quarry rises in the air and we shoot. Then he retrieves and gently delivers the fowl to our hands.

"We can determine exactly which one of these types of bird dogs a hunter owns just by observing the pair after a day's hunting. The owner of 'You Go First' gloomily drags the dog from the box while anxiously looking around to see whether any neighbors are watching. The owner of 'See You in the Next County' never returned from the hunt at all. He's still out looking for his dog. (Some owners only search for 'See You in the Next County' on the slim chance of trading for 'Mr. Perfection.')

"After the owner releases him from the dog box, 'Mr. Perfection' sits on the tailgate while each bird is slowly and deliberately removed from the hunting vest and carefully arranged in a row in front of the proud animal. Neighbors are called over, pictures are taken, and congratulations are given. Finally, the 'kennel' command is given and 'Mr. Perfection' jumps down from the tailgate, and with head and tail held high, prances to the kennel, hops on the doghouse and stretches out with a dreamy look in his eyes."

Alfred assures me he has never owned a bird dog that wasn't "Mr. Perfection."

9

Old Sam and Me: A Match Made in Heaven

I'm not sure he understands every word, but I have a friend who listens to a lot of my tales when we're out on the road together. Old Sam and I go back nine years now and I can't imagine life without him, even though I know he won't be with me much longer.

It is theorized that all dogs descended from a prehistoric animal called *Tomarctus*. *Tomarctus* looked somewhat like a wolf with a thick coat, a tail, and a wedge-shaped head. Descendants of *Tomarctus* became the family *Canidae* that includes all the world's wolves, coyotes, jackals, foxes, and dogs.

Researchers believe man first saw the advantage of adopting dogs as hunting partners around twelve thousand years ago. Nomadic hunters who lived in what is now Europe befriended dogs and taught them to track game. The reward for the dog was, of course, a share of the kill.

It was a partnership that was meant to be. Many researchers believe we would have been slower in becoming the advanced civilization we are today if it weren't for the help of our canine friends. For countless generations the dog, in return for food and love, has acted as a hunting partner, a hard working farm hand, a transporter, a rescuer, a courageous protector and above all, a loyal, loving friend who stays by his master's side in the best and worst of times, never straying from the bond as humans are known to do.

I first became fascinated with dogs as a young boy while following my dad and Uncle Sam Moore on quail hunting excursions.

They made such an imprint on a young boy, those old bird dogs, long since gone. It was such a joy to watch them bounding through fields with unremitting vigor, so eager to please their master.

I can't remember not having a dog or two or three around the house. English setters were Daddy's favorite, but through the years, we owned Irish setters, golden retrievers, a chihuahua, and a Saint Bernard.

Most people who have owned dogs all their lives can recall one that stands out, the dog that was far more intelligent than the rest, the best hunter, the one that lived the longest, or maybe the one that saved a life. Of all the dogs I have ever owned, one dog certainly stands out from the rest, and he's the one still with me today, old Sam.

Dave and His Right-Hand Man, Sam

I am convinced that an unknown force was at work the day Sam and I first met. He was a three-month-old among a remnant litter of four or five pups. When the breeder took me outside to pick one, Sam approached me, leaving the other pups behind. With eyes that would melt anyone's heart, he looked up at me as if to say, "I thought you would never get here."

On the way home that day, Sam repeatedly licked me on the face as I drove down the highway. It was his first trip in a vehicle, and you'd think he'd be frightened, or at the very least, uneasy. But not Sam. It was as if he were elated that his master was finally taking him home. This was a match made in heaven.

By the time Sam was two years old, we had become as close as a dog and a human could be. My wife Diann, who wasn't much of a dog lover before, had fallen in love with him as well. "He understands almost every word we say. I've never seen a dog like him before," she'd tell me.

We took Sam everywhere with us: to family reunions, vacations, fishing trips, and even work. Seldom did people see us without Sam by our side. My dad has often commented that Sam is the world's most loved animal.

At the age of four Sam was at the prime of life and enjoying every minute of it when his world and ours was nearly turned upside down. Diann and I had been experiencing a marital crisis, and one winter night a terrible fight left us both wondering if our marriage had any chance at all. At some point during the night both of us managed to drift off to sleep with Sam at the foot of our bed, as always. It was during this time that Sam did something so astonishing that no one will ever be able to explain it.

When I awoke the next morning about daybreak and saw him there, I was flabbergasted. Sam was lying on the floor with his head positioned in the crease of our opened wedding album, looking at me with those big sad eyes. Sometime during the wee hours of the morning he had gone to a nearby coffee table and removed a stack of books, one by one, until he reached the bottom of the layer, where our wedding album lay. He then carried the album to the foot of the bed, opened it, laid his head in it, and waited for me to awaken.

Why did he do it? Was it sheer coincidence? Were there forces working through him? Or do some dogs understand more than we give them credit for?

Diann and I managed to work through our crisis. But I'm not sure we would be together today if it weren't for Sam's mysterious act. Before the sun crept above the horizon that cold winter morning I looked at every page of the wedding album Sam had opened for me, reminded of the beautiful woman I had married. And I cannot count the times I have recalled the image of Sam lying there with those woeful eyes, as if he were pleading with me to come to my senses and keep the pack together.

Today, Diann and I are happier than ever with a beautiful daughter named Miranda, who may owe her very existence to an old dog named Sam.

At the age of five Sam made his first appearance on *Kentucky Afield*. He eventually became my co-host, a position that would give him enormous popularity. Sam is certainly not pretentious in his television role. Most of the time when he's seen with me out on location or by my side as I open the show, he usually struggles to stay awake. Sam and Duke of the old *Beverly Hillbillies* TV show are very much alike. Perhaps it is this laid-back manner that people like so much. Whatever it is, Sam is now upstaging his own master. He has tens of thousands of loyal fans, many of whom write him letters. And many of the people who write me want to know all about Sam. Even a hair from his furry coat is a hot item. The following is an excerpt from a recent letter written by Ms. Johnnie Davis of Benton, Kentucky.

> "Thanks for autographing the *Kentucky Afield* hat we received . . . I wanted to share a short story with you about our receiving it . . . As my husband unpackaged the hat . . . the whole neighborhood probably heard my 12 year-old daughter Amanda's excited squeals . . . Then she and John, her 10 year-old brother, closely inspected the hat, looking for a hair off Sam . . ."

Sam Signing Autographs

By the time Sam reached his eighth year he was a veteran traveler and outdoor television personality. By now I had begun to lose track of all the back roads he and I had journeyed upon.

In the summer of 1992 one such journey took us to the rugged mountainous country of eastern Kentucky. The other members of the *Kentucky Afield* staff were scattered elsewhere in a state that spans more than five hundred miles from east to west.

On this trip I was "one-man-banding" a segment for the show. With such a small staff, sometimes we have to take on a project alone and play the multi-faceted role of producer, cameraman, and even on-air talent. That is, if we can get ourselves in frame with the help of a tripod.

Sam and I had come to a land of densely forested mountains, tall cliffs, and natural arches. We were there to shoot some scenes for a segment on the history of wildlife restoration in America. Conservation Officers Bill Jolly and Dale McKensie soon arrived to lend a hand in hauling camera equipment through that rugged terrain, as well as to lend me their knowledge of the topic.

A couple of hours into the shoot I noticed Sam had wandered about seventy-five yards up the mountain to its summit, where he was sitting on a boulder. I figured he must have been having a wonderful time. He was actually awake and had been for at least an hour!

About fifteen minutes later I looked up at that boulder to check on him, but he was gone. At first I wasn't alarmed, just a little surprised. Sam never likes to leave sight of me.

"Here, Sam! Come on, boy!" I shouted.

But he didn't return. At that point I decided to walk up to the top of the mountain to see what that old dog was up to. When I reached the top and saw what was on the other side of the boulder he'd been sitting on, a dreadful feeling overtook me. He was perched on the edge of a fifty-foot cliff!

"Hey fellows, I think something bad might have happened to Sam!" I shouted down to Bill and Dale.

"He's more than likely chasing some critter!" Dale yelled back.

I prayed that Dale was right, even though Sam had never chased anything for more than a few yards.

Bill and Dale must have had their doubts about that possibility, too. Both of them began to make their way around the hill to the bottom of the cliff. In the meantime I called and called for the friend who had been by my side for eight years.

Bill and Dale found no sign of Sam at the bottom of the cliff, an immeasurable relief. But where was he? What had this wilderness done to him?

As darkness approached, the three of us had walked and climbed and called to the limits of human endurance.

"I can't thank you fellows enough for helping me, but it's time for y'all to go on home to your wives and kids, and your own dogs. I'll stay out here for a while longer," I told Bill and Dale. The two of them had owned dogs all of their lives. They knew what I was going through, the feeling of loss, almost as if it were a son or daughter lost out there. With worried looks on their faces Bill and Dale headed down the mountain to their vehicle, assuring me they'd be back at first light if need be.

I called to Sam until twilight faded into darkness, still holding on to the thread of hope that, as unlike him as it was, he would suddenly come bounding through the woods, tired and thirsty after running a critter all day. But it didn't happen. Brokenhearted, I sat on the boulder where I had last seen him, and in the dark of that night, as the whippoorwill and the owl began their lonesome calls, it finally dawned on me that Sam was probably gone forever. The two hour, heartwrenching trip home was one I'll never forget.

When I got home in the pre-dawn hours, I broke the news to Diann that Sam had disappeared high on top of a mountain. The dog that had made such an impact on our lives was either dead or lost. Both of us feared that if he was lost, he may eventually wind up in the hands of unscrupulous humans, much the way Buck did in Jack London's *The Call of the Wild*. The thought of Sam being abused was horrifying.

The next morning I drove back to the mountains where Sam had vanished. I stopped at some of the few houses in that isolated country, hanging on to a tiny shred of optimism. Someone may have seen him. Thank goodness something told me to knock on one last door before heading back home.

"Sir, have you seen a golden retriever around here?" I asked the elderly gentleman who came to the door.
"Nawh, ain't seen a dog. But I tell ya' what I heard this mornin' 'fore daylight. It was the most mournful howlin' I ever heard, like a lonesome wolf. It went on for the longest time,

right up there on that mountain. I knew that critter had to be mighty sad."

"Thank you, sir. You don't know how much I appreciate that information. I can't thank you enough," I said.

"You're welcome, son. Slow down now," he shouted, as I dashed toward my truck.

With a new feeling of hope I sped away to the base of the mountain, then hiked up toward that boulder as fast as my legs could carry me. Pausing to catch my breath before reaching the summit, I looked up at the boulder. To my amazement, there he was! Overwhelmed with joy I shouted, "Sam, come down here!" Obviously he was overjoyed, as well, as he made his way toward me, whimpering the whole way. It was a greeting that can't be described in words. He practically licked the skin off my face. I'm sure I hugged him harder than he'd ever been hugged in his life. We were re-united after a traumatic separation.

That was the first time I've seen a dog smile. I had always heard that some dogs are capable of smiling when they are overwhelmed with happiness, but I wasn't sure how true that was until I saw it with my own eyes. They show their teeth, which creates nearly the same expression they have when they're growling.

Sam had obviously fallen from one of the cliffs along the top of that mountain. His head was swollen and knotted, and for days afterward he was very slow in getting up, probably from soreness. I can only guess what happened.

Perhaps he fell a short distance, enough to knock him unconscious, or at least disorient him, which would explain why he never came to us when we called. We could have nearly stepped on him during that search. If that is what happened, when he finally came to his senses, I was gone. Then he likely began howling. And that moanful howl did just what it was supposed to do in an indirect way. He was trying to tell his long lost master where he was. Even though I heard it secondhand, the primordial call of the canine served its timeless purpose.

Months passed, and the spring of 1993 was upon us. For me, thirty-five was right around the corner. For the first time in my life I was noticing how quickly birthdays arrive each year. Sam was fast approaching nine, which in human years would make him a senior citizen.

Although he's a bit arthritic and somewhat slower than he was in the old days, Sam is always ready for a romp in the creek. And after a seemingly endless winter of frigid hunting and fishing I had developed a bad case of wet legging fever by mid-April: no layered clothing, no winter coveralls, and no waders. What a nice change of pace it would be.

On a crystal clear spring afternoon Sam and I headed to Elkhorn Creek in north-central Kentucky, one of the finest streams for smallmouth bass in the southeastern United States. The shallow, clear pools and ripples of Elkhorn can take on an entirely different appearance after heavy rains. On this day the creek looked more like the Colorado River. I should have headed back home at the first sight of the stream, but like an illicit drug, my fishing addiction was overpowering me.

For a while Sam and I walked the banks as I looked for calm eddies where smallmouth bass might be hiding. Usually it is a struggle to keep Sam out of the water until I fish a hole out, but on this occasion he was making no attempt to go for a swim. I should have paid attention to his animal instinct, for he knew the current was too swift. But visions of a three-pound smallie dancing on the water were all I could see.

Rushing water can be dangerously deceptive. The section of stream I decided to cross to reach an eddy looked to be about knee deep, but I soon discovered it wasn't. The raging current quickly caught me at waist level. Suddenly, I was struggling to stand up against such a powerful force.

Sam was watching me from the bank, and just as I lost my footing he leaped in front of me. I remember grabbing his neck and feeling his powerful thrusts as he tried to pull me to the bank. But his gallant effort was futile. The current continued to carry us both downstream. Fortunately, the raging torrents of the Elkhorn are usually short-lived, and within a few seconds we found ourselves in calmer waters.

Even though he failed to pull me to shore it was the thought that counts. Sam was willing to risk his life to save his master's. And if I were going to drown, he was going with me.

BACK TRAILS & FISHING TALES

Sometimes I look at him, thinking of all the years we've had together and the experiences we've shared, and I realize just how fortunate I am to have a friend like old Sam.

Some may think of dogs as dumb creatures unworthy of human kindness, but dogs and man were meant for each other, as those nomadic hunters discovered so long ago. Down through the ages stories have been told of extraordinary friendships between canine and human, as if, every now and then, a match was made in heaven. So it was with old Sam and me.

Artist's Rendition of Sam's Rescue Attempt

10

Stream Fishin' for Smallies

The rushing water pours over thousands of rounded rocks, large and small. The sound alone has a soothing, refreshing effect. I begin to wade out into the cool waters of the riffle, occasionally slipping on rocks as slick as glass. I have to get closer to the calmer eddy on the far side of the stream. As I reach the midpoint I can tell the eddy looks like a perfect hiding place for a smallmouth bass. I toss a Rapala minnow imitator into the eddy just beyond the rapid. I twitch my rod, which causes the lure to dance erratically on the surface. I wait several seconds and twitch it again. Suddenly the water swirls below the lure, and a smallmouth blasts out of the water and engulfs the lure, creating a small explosion! Now I'm on a high no drug could ever duplicate. I feel an adrenaline rush as the big bass doubles over my ultra-light rod. The fight is on! With a mighty leap the fish breaks the surface and becomes an aerial acrobat as he violently tries to shake the lure out of his mouth. Now he heads for the rapid.

The drag on my spinning reel is pulling hard, as I am now fighting both the current and the fish! At this point I simply try to hang on and hope he wears down soon. A few seconds later his strength is beginning to wane. I walk him back to the eddy, where I can reel him in without dealing with the rapid. Finally, I pull the exhausted two-pound bass from the water, look at him eye to eye, and think to myself, "I won this battle, but you put up one heckuva fight." With needle-nose pliers I remove the treble hook from his mouth and gently release him back into the water.

That scenario was not a dream sequence or a fictitious moment in my imagination. I have lived it time and time again. My love for stream fishing only seems to get stronger with each passing year.

In each book I write, I plan to include a chapter about an aspect of sport hunting or fishing that I have become so involved in and fascinated with that I can write about the subject with a lot of heart, and perhaps a tiny bit of authority.

For this edition I have chosen stream fishing for smallmouth bass. As echoed throughout this book, my passion for stream fishing first came about as a toddler on Green River, a nationally renowned smallmouth stream mentioned in publications such as *McClane's Standard Fishing Encyclopedia*. I can look back on endless memories of rushing riffles, the crashing sound of jon-boats being dragged across them, the long deep holes so still they yield a mirror image of enormous overhanging sycamore trees seemingly as ancient as the river itself, and countless recollections of those jumping, dancing, fighting smallmouth bass.

In many parts of the United States, river and stream smallmouth fishing is a little known opportunity. While the lakes get all the fishing pressure, an angler can hop in a canoe or jon-boat, or put on a pair of waders, and enjoy a stream without worrying about encountering a crowd. But it is certainly advantageous to know what type of river or stream to look for. A moderate gradient stream with a mixture of riffles, shallow pools, and deep holes is ideal for smallmouth. Low country streams with slow-moving currents and silty bottoms are not conducive to smallmouth, nor are high gradient streams that have too much fast-flowing water. Look for something in between these extremes.

Although stream and river smallmouth are generally not quite as large as those that inhabit the big lakes (a four-pound stream smallie is a whopper in anyone's book), they will fight just as hard, if not harder, than the bigger lake residents. This may be due to the fact that stream smallmouth have lived their entire lives fighting currents.

Ultra-light gear is my preference when fishing streams. There's nothing like the feel of a fighting smallmouth when you catch him on a light rod and reel. And lighter gear makes it easier to cast smaller baits and lures that smallmouth like. Today, an angler can be overwhelmed by the plethora of this type of equipment available to him. I prefer spinning outfits, although I do not claim to be enough of an expert to say these are absolutely the best. Whatever feels most comfortable to you and can give you the most confidence is the right choice when it comes to equipment.

If there's one thing life experience has taught me, however, it is that you get what you pay for when it comes to equipment. Trying to save a few bucks by buying a cheap outfit, whatever the type, will get you nowhere in a hurry. Good performance is either short-lived or non-existent.

The type of monofilament line one uses is another important element of stream fishing for smallies. I normally use low visibility, four to six-pound test line. If I'm in a stream with a big population of smaller fish, I'll stick with four-pound line. But if I'm fishing a stream known for occasional monsters, I'll move up to stronger six-pound line. Clear, colored line is my normal preference for streams. However, I have recently discovered a camouflage color that is virtually invisible underwater.

Some of my favorite artificial baits are Rapala floating minnow imitators, A.C. Shiner minnow imitators, Rebel crayfish imitators, Heddon Tiny Torpedo propeller lures, small spinners such as the one-eighth ounce Rooster Tails and number two Mepps spinners, various shallow running crankbaits, and curly-tail grubs on lead-head jigs. If I'm wade fishing, I carry just enough of these baits to fill up a miniature tackle box that will fit in the large pockets of my fishing vest. It's simply impractical to carry a bulky tackle box while wading a stream.

A Fighting Smallmouth Taken from Elkhorn Creek

Dave and Friends After a Rabbit Hunt

Kentucky Fish & Wildlife Commissioner Don McCormick, Dave, and Videographer Alfred Fields After a Crappie Show on Lake Barkley

Dave; His Dad, Billy; His Sister, Marilyn, a Guidance Counselor; and His Brother, Bill, a Plastic Surgeon

Bald Eagle at Ballard Wildlife Management Area

A View of Big South Fork National River

Snowy Mountains of the Appalachians

Ballard Wildlife Management Area in Western Kentucky – Kentucky's Own Version of Louisiana Swamps

Dave One-Man-Banding

Dave Filming at Dix River, One of Kentucky's Spectacular Cliff-lined Streams

*Dave's Near Thirty-Pound Freshwater Drum,
Not Far Off the State Record*

A Kentucky Lake Scene at Sunrise

Some of Dave's Favorite Stream Fishing Baits

Reeling in a Smallie

Smallmouth will readily take any of these artificial baits, and then some. The secret is finding out where to throw them. If you can find a riffle with quiet pockets and eddies adjacent to it, you are looking at a smallmouth hangout. Smallmouth wait in these calmer waters for their prey to wash downstream in the riffle or rapid. When they spot a potential meal, they dart out into the rushing water and ambush it. Throw a bait into the eddy where they're waiting and hang on. The same principle applies to areas just above and just below riffles. I like to think of a riffle or rapid as potentially surrounded by fish.

When I'm wade fishing I try to angle my casts somewhat upstream whenever possible, because the fish normally face upstream as they wait for their prey to drift toward them. Also, when a lure is thrown downstream in faster moving water its action is often adversely affected by the heavy current as it is reeled in.

When faster moving water comes in contact with obstructions such as boulders or logs, eddies are found on the back side of them as well. I keep an eye out for such places because smallmouth can be found holding in the eddy.

In the deep, calm stretches I prefer to tie on something that can get down to the bottom, such as a curly-tail grub with a lead head. Smallmouth don't stay in the shallows around riffles. They go there to feed, then return to the depths to rest. A resting fish near the bottom needs a little more enticement than a surface or shallow running lure. But drop a grub in front of his face and it's a new ballgame. A black curly-tail grub with a weedless lead head bounced on the bottom under a root wad landed me one of the biggest stream smallmouth I've ever caught, a hefty three-pounder. The one irritating problem I have encountered while grub fishing is that of my "skirt being pulled down." In other words, the grub has a tendency to slip off the collar of the lead head when a fish strikes at it or when it hits a snag, and the angler pulls loose. To help solve this problem, I have recently begun carrying a lighter to heat the collar of the lead head before putting on the grub. The hot collar will melt the plastic somewhat, causing it to adhere to the lead.

Dave Enjoying the Extra Benefits of Stream Fishing: Spectacular Scenery

Deep holes are also the spots I prefer to use live bait. Smallmouth move to the deep holes to rest after feeding in the shallows and during the winter months when they're not feeding much at all. In these situations, even though a curly-tail grub can often prompt a strike, live bait is the ultimate answer. The reason is simple. When live bait is dangled under their nose it is an easy meal they don't have to expend much energy to get. And you can't beat the look of live bait. After all, it's real. Even the best artificial bait ever made cannot completely duplicate a live creature.

Baits such as minnows, crayfish, crickets, and nightcrawlers are fine choices, but the most productive live bait I have ever used for smallmouth is the hellgrammite. Smallmouth love them.

A hellgrammite (sometimes called go-devil) is the larval stage of a dobsonfly. You can find these creatures under rocks in riffles. If you are fishing alone, tie a minnow seine to two sticks, find a riffle and face downstream, spread the net out in front of you, anchoring the sticks into the stream bed, and then kick up the rocks with your feet. Two anglers can share the duties as one holds the net and the other lifts up the rocks. It may take several attempts to get enough hellgrammites for a day's fishing.

Although hellgrammites are hardy and seem to live indefinitely, it's a good idea to keep them in a container with a little water, some small rocks and pebbles, and some moss or other aquatic vegetation. For wade fishing, the angler should consider a practical way to carry the bait. I like the coffee can method. Simply punch two holes in a coffee can so a small rope can be inserted into each hole and knotted, enabling you to throw the rope over your shoulder. I'm sure there are better methods, but if you drink as much coffee as I do you wind up with coffee cans all over the house. Sometimes it takes some creative thinking to figure out what to do with them all.

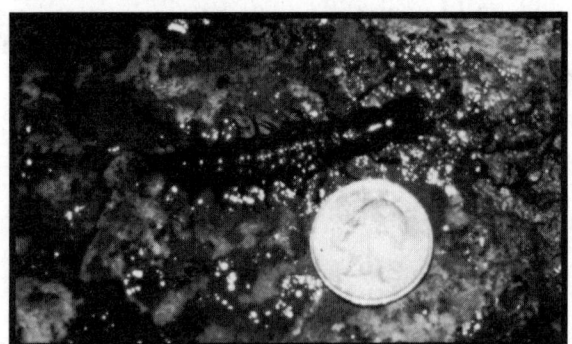

A Hellgrammite (quarter shown for size comparison)

I prefer a number four or six hook when using hellgrammites. The hellgrammite has an armor-like collar near its head. I like to slide the hook under and out this collar, which keeps the hook away from any vital areas. The process of hooking a hellgrammite should be undertaken with a degree of caution. A healthy three-inch hellgrammite has a pair of mandibles that can pinch the daylights out of a finger. I learned my lesson the hard way!

With a couple of split-shot sinkers eighteen inches or so up your line, you are ready to fish your hellgrammite.

One problem I have encountered with hellgrammite fishing is hang-ups. After all that seining it is frustrating to lose a healthy hellgrammite that was just put on the hook. Noted wildlife cinematographer and stream fisherman Karl Maslowski told me the way he avoids this annoyance is through the use of a bobber. The bobber keeps his hellgrammite suspended just above the bottom, avoiding snags. I had always thought hellgrammites should be fished on the bottom. Once I tried Karl's bobber method I quickly found out that fish will take the hellgrammite just as readily.

Fishing with live bait is a little trickier than fishing with artificial bait. Smallmouth often mouth the bait before finally deciding to take it. This is often the case in deep water where fish are not as aggressive as they are in the shallows. When I see my bobber go under, I wait a few seconds before setting the hook. Although it is tough to control the urge to set the hook the instant the bobber goes under, waiting will give the fish time to completely take the bait.

Scientists are still learning about the sensory capabilities of smallmouth, but it doesn't take a science book to find out how easily they're spooked. Thrashing around in the water while wade fishing, and actions such as tossing the paddle in the bottom of the boat send clear signals to smallmouth to get the heck out of the area.

When I'm wade fishing, I move as slowly and cautiously as possibly. When I spot an eddy, I'll stay back as far as possible and cast the maximum distance to reach it, trying not to spook the fish. When the water is exceptionally clear I wear earth-tone clothing, and sometimes camouflage. A smallmouth can see a bright red cap or shirt a good distance away in shallow, clear water. I've even been known to wrap camouflage tape around my live bait coffee can.

Kentucky is blessed with more miles of rivers and streams than any state other than Alaska. So, it's hard not to get into stream fishing if you're a Kentuckian. But no matter what part of the country you live in, a stream is usually within driving distance.

If my methods of stream fishing don't sound appealing, you might consider fly fishing, which is not only an effective way to catch fish, but also an art form.

If you are a newcomer to the sport of stream fishing I strongly recommend going with someone who is familiar with the sport for the first few excursions. And, of course, don't be afraid to ask questions. I shutter to think how many thousands of stream fishing questions I've asked Fisheries Biologist and stream angler Ted Crowell. I often wonder if I worry him to death, but he assures me I don't. Ted says he's more than happy to pass on his knowledge of stream fishing to me or anyone else who has the desire to take up the sport. I believe my good friend Ted has the right attitude.

If you take up stream fishing, you'll soon find that you are getting a multitude of benefits all at the same time: the enjoyment of sport fishing without a major investment in a lake bass boat, the pleasure of seeing wildlife along the stream corridor, and good exercise. Even on float trips I periodically stop to wade. So put on that old fishing vest, grab a fishing pole, and head up a creek.

11

A Tradition Worth Keeping

As the saying goes, "Times are a-changin'." Today's America bears little resemblance to the America our fathers knew back in the 1940's and `50's. For the last decade hunting license sales have been on a decline. And fishing license sales are beginning to level off. Many factors enter into this trend. One of these factors is that so many children today living in single parent homes are not being exposed to hunting and fishing. And urbanization has resulted in millions of people, young and old, losing all contact with hunting, fishing, and nature in general.

Competing recreational pursuits such as golf, tennis, television, electronic games, and a myriad of other opportunities have also cut into the numbers of hunters and fishermen. While these societal changes take place, license sales and excise taxes on hunting and fishing equipment continue to pay the bulk of the cost of wildlife and fisheries restoration and management in America.

It may sound ironic to non-sportsmen that hunters and fishermen, the consumptive users, pay for the restoration of our fish and wildlife resources. But modern day hunting and fishing is highly regulated with seasons, limits, and continuous scientific monitoring. Today's sportsmen do not adversely affect fish and wildlife populations, nor do they have the desire to do so. A good example of a huntable wildlife species is the eastern cottontail rabbit, an animal in no danger of becoming extinct. In fact, the cottontail is so prolific that a single pair, along with their offspring, could produce 350,000 rabbits within five years if no young were lost to predation, according to the *Audubon Society Field Guide to North American Mammals.* Yet it is the sportsmen's money that pays for the restoration of species whose numbers are adversely affected by factors such as loss of habitat and pollution.

This is a critical time in the history of the conservation movement. I believe those of us who are sportsmen and wildlife enthusiasts should make a special effort to expose our children to the great outdoors, not merely for reasons of sustaining funding for wildlife restoration, but because exposure to hunting, fishing, and nature builds character, patience, and knowledge of our natural environment. And some traditions are simply worthy of preservation. What's wrong with carrying on something our father did, and his father before him?

Sometimes I go back home to the banks of the Green to be alone. It is a good place to ponder the past and the future. For this old river has withstood the ages, a constant in a world that changes from day to day. And old man river will likely roll on for ages to come, touching lives just the way he always has down through the countless generations. My daughter, Miranda, is still too young to comprehend the natural world around her. But it won't be long now until she can join me in the grand outdoors I have come to love so dearly.

A Budding Outdoor Writer?

I pray she will be with her daddy on that old river when the grey squirrel bounds along the limb of an ancient sycamore tree. May her eyes, wide with wonder, capture the noble stance of the great blue herron. May she hear the melody of a dozen songbirds and feel the ferocity of a smallmouth bass. May she never take these things for granted. And may she recall, and her children after her, a pact made on a battlefield in Belgium a long time ago.

FOR ADDITIONAL COPIES OF
BACK TRAILS & FISHING TALES
DAVE SHUFFETT'S OUTDOOR ADVENTURES

Write: **Antex Corporation**
120 Dennis Drive
Lexington, KY 40503
Phone/Fax: (800) 982-7623

Send me _____ copies at $12.95 per copy plus shipping charge of $3.00 for the first copy and $1.50 shipping for each additional copy. VISA and MasterCard accepted.

Name: _____

Address: _____

City: _____ State: _____ Zip: _____

Card #:_____

Total Enclosed: $_____ (KY residents add 6% sales tax)

Make check or money order payable to Antex Corporation

FOR ADDITIONAL COPIES OF
BACK TRAILS & FISHING TALES
DAVE SHUFFETT'S OUTDOOR ADVENTURES

Write: **Antex Corporation**
120 Dennis Drive
Lexington, KY 40503
Phone/Fax: (800) 982-7623

Send me _____ copies at $12.95 per copy plus shipping charge of $3.00 for the first copy and $1.50 shipping for each additional copy. VISA and MasterCard accepted.

Name: _____

Address: _____

City: _____ State: _____ Zip: _____

Card #:_____

Total Enclosed: $_____ (KY residents add 6% sales tax)
Make check or money order payable to Antex Corporation

Also Available from Antex

First Love: A Story About Basketball -- A basketball player's reflections on growing up in Kentucky playing basketball.

Richie -- Former University of Kentucky basketball player Richie Farmer tells of his storied basketball career.

Children's Products

Alphabet Alive: *A Letter Safari* -- 392 pages of fun, educational activities, including: puppet patterns, poems, word searches, songs, and more!

Alphabet Alive: *Classroom Creations* -- Fantastic, new manipulative activity book for educational use.

Class Acts: *Plays, Skits, & Dramas* -- Exciting, new plays, skits, and dramas for classroom, school, or church use.

Nosey Rides the Train -- The tale of a cute, little basset hound whose curiosity takes him on a train ride far from home.

Wee-Dolph, The Tiniest Reindeer -- A lovable children's book with beautiful color pictures telling the story of the tiniest reindeer of all.

Find these & other Antex publications where books are sold.

Antex Corporation
Lexington, KY
1-800-982-7623

To order these Antex publications please fill out and mail this form to:

Antex Corporation
120 Dennis Dr.
Lexington, KY 40503

Or use your VISA or MasterCard and call or fax your order at 1-800-982-7623.

Quantity
__First Love: A Story About Basketball $9.95 (+$2.50 S&H)

__Richie $9.95 (+$2.50 S&H)
__Richie -- *Blue Letter Edition* $14.95 (+$2.50 S&H)

__Alphabet Alive: A Letter Safari $24.95 (+$4.00 S&H)

__Alphabet Alive: Classroom Creation $12.95 (+$3.50 S&H)

__Class Acts: Plays, Skits, & Dramas $9.95 (+$3.00 S&H)

__Nosey Rides the Train $3.95 (+$1.50 S&H)

__Wee-Dolph: The Tiniest Reindeer $8.95 (+$3.00 S&H)

Total Enclosed: $_____   (KY residents add 6% sales tax)

Make Check or Money Order payable to Antex Corporation.